EVALUATING FOR EXCELLENCE

HANS A. ANDREWS

Illinois Valley Community College

NEW FORUMS PRESS, INC.

Stillwater, Oklahoma 74076

Library of Congress Catalog Card Number 84-062727

ISBN 0-913507-04-0

This book is available at a special discount when ordered in bulk quantities. For information, contact New Forums Press, Inc., P.O. Box 876, Stillwater, OK 74076.

Printed in the United States of America.

"The ultimate winner or loser in our struggle for excellence is our student when we're teaching . . ."

John E. Roueche

In Memory of Tony Baron

Contents

Preface

THE CENTRAL THEME of this book is that boards of education, trustees, administrators and faculty leaders can and should work together to insure that a decade of dedication to "excellence in instruction" will occur in American and Canadian secondary schools, community, junior, and technical colleges, and four-year colleges and universities.

The tremendous growth in high school enrollments, new community, technical, and junior colleges, and expanded four-year colleges and university campuses in both the United States and Canada during the 1960s and 1970s is behind us. Left behind in the dust of this period of fast growth are some areas in the educational system which have been *neglected* while other priorities were being met. The whole process of faculty evaluation and faculty development is in disarray. At a time when critical studies of American education are pointing to a decline in student test scores, lower student achievement, and deficiencies in basic educational skills, educators are finally beginning to realize that they do not have a framework developed with adequate procedures to *guarantee* their students quality and excellence in the classroom.

This writer believes strongly that excellence can and

must be expected but *cannot be assumed* without an effective *administrative evaluation system* for faculty. This book is dedicated to all practitioners in the field of faculty evaluation . . . to boards of education, boards of trustees, superintendents and principals of secondary schools, college presidents, vice presidents and deans of instruction, division and department chairpersons who do so much of the work in the trenches, and to faculty who want excellence in their classrooms, and to all students who enter the educational system expecting to receive quality instruction in every class in which they enroll.

The author intends to present a comprehensive framework for an administrative *faculty evaluation system* to be developed starting with (1) Evaluating for Excellence: Defining a "Straw Person" and the Total Job Parameters; (2) "Negotiating" and "Modeling" Away Board Responsibilities to Evaluate; (3) Determining Qualifications and Competencies of Faculty; (4) Board of Trustee Policies in the Development of An Administrative Evaluation System; (5) Evaluating "Non-Tenured" Faculty; (6) Evaluating the "Untouchables"—Tenured Faculty; (7) The Legal and Competency Needs of Academic Administrators; (8) Guiding the Evaluator: Positive Evaluation; (9) Rewarding Excellence in Instruction; (10) Guiding the Evaluator: Negative Evaluations; (11) Guiding the Board: Some Practical Discussion on Preparing a Notice to Remedy; (12) Guiding the Board: Preparing for Just Cause Dismissals of Faculty; (13) Conclusion.

I wish to express my thanks to those persons who have helped formulate the theme and contents for this book. Mr. W. H. Judd (deceased), my original mentor who encouraged experimentation and creativity in working with students while not sacrificing quality; Dr. Ralph C. Bedell, Professor Emeritus, University of Missouri-Columbia, for his guidance and encouragement for the past 15 years; Dr. Richard F. Whitmore and Floyd Oglesby who provided a climate of growth in developing quality programs at Kellogg Community College in Battle Creek, Michigan, and to Dr. Alfred Wisgoski, President of Illinois Valley Community College, and the I.V.C.C. Board of Trustees who expected, encouraged, and supported the development of a strong and effective administrative evaluation system.

I am also very grateful to Mr. Bruce Mackey whose legal counsel has greatly assisted me through some very trying times. In top priority, I wish to thank my wife, Carolyn, for her encouragement in attempting this endeavor after living with my highs and lows in the rewarding of merit recognition or in the dismissal of incompetent instructors over the years. Special thanks goes to Nancy Querciagrossa for her superb work in editing and preparing the many phases of the manuscript on the word processor. A special note of thanks also goes to Evelyn Moyle for her unending research assistance in obtaining obscure materials as asked.

The Author

HANS A. ANDREWS is Dean of Instruction of Illinois Valley Community College. His Bachelor's of Science degree (1960) was earned at Central Michigan University in Business Education. His Master's in Arts degree in Counseling and Guidance was earned at Michigan State University (1963), and his Ed. D. degree (1971) from the University of Missouri-Columbia in Counseling Psychology.

Andrews' professional roles in community colleges have been primarily in administration. His present role as instructional Dean at Illinois Valley Community College was preceded by several years as Vice President for Community and Students Services, Dean of Community Services, Evening College Dean, and Evening College Counselor all at Kellogg Community College in Michigan. Andrews has published 18 professional articles in the following publications: *Community and Junior College Journal; The Journal of Staff, Program, & Organization Development; School Business Affairs; Community College Frontiers; The Community Services Catalyst; The Journal of Student Financial Aid; Community Education Journal; Journal of Vocational Behavior;* and *Journal of Counseling Psychology.*

Andrews' other professional commitments include being a member of the editorial board of the *Catalyst.* He is president of the executive board of the National Council of Community Services and Continuing Education for 1984-1985.

In addition to his roles in dealing with evaluation at the community college level, Dr. Andrews spent five years as a teacher and Director of Guidance in Michigan High Schools. In dedicating a yearbook to Dr. Andrews in his second year of teaching, his students his students referred to him as "a friend, counselor, and teacher extraordinaire."

Foreword

THE CONCEPT OF FACULTY EVALUATION has evolved from being a threat to becoming a common and expected occurrence. Whereas faculty and administrators often looked at evaluation as something done by others to them—almost in a "Big Brother" stance—they now may perceive the action in a positive light as a way of enhancing their own performance.

Fifteen years ago, measuring faculty performance might vary from college to college, but it was consistent in that it was employed by all institutions in one form or another. Although district policies might mandate evaluation, the techniques employed and the potential utilization of findings were often criticized by the instructors themselves. The use of various rating scales by supervisors and colleagues, by students, and by grants and degrees all had something to say about instructional practices. Rating by self might be considered the most mature, most effective, and most permanent way of judging, but this procedure was seldom employed.

Now Dr. Andrews, a dean of instruction who is familiar

with all types of administrator and instructor evaluation, presents a contemporary view of the issues involved. Evaluation, viewed previously as a potential negative, is now perceived as a matter of course. Dean Andrews discusses evaluation in terms of boards of trustees, unions, administration, legal considerations, and the guidance of evaluators. He brings a fresh, yet scholarly and thoughtful, approach to the necessary, sometimes mundane role of evaluation. And, he considers the various procedures in light of excellence, presenting ways in which evaluation can better effect not only the instructors and administrators but the total environment of community colleges, universities, and public schools.

At a time when collective bargaining is popular; when questions of legality prevail; and when retention, accountability, and effectiveness are prevalent issues, Dr. Andrews has written a timely book. We recommend this text as important reading for community college administrators and faculty members, school principals, university professors of higher education, and members of boards of trustees.

Arthur M. Cohen

President, Center for
the Study of Community
Colleges; Professor of Higher
Education, UCLA; Director
of the ERIC Clearinghouse for
Junior Colleges, UCLA

Florence B. Brawer

Research Director, Center for
the Study of Community
Colleges; Staff Associate, ERIC
Clearinghouse for Junior
Colleges, UCLA

1

"Of chief concern in the process of teaching is the potential growth of each student."
—Laura L. Nash, 1982

Evaluating For Excellence: Defining a "Strawperson" and the Total Job Parameters

AN ADMINISTRATIVE FACULTY EVALUATION system has to be proposed as a viable and credible means of strengthening educational institutions. The smokescreen that has so long prevailed and has kept secondary schools and colleges from seriously considering administrative evaluation must be lifted.

Education has received its report card in the mid-1980s and it leaves much to be desired. No less than five national studies have pointed to the serious decline in student test scores, a major decline in academic requirements for students prior to entering college, and concern relative to preparation or persons entering teaching and other professions. The President of the United States, in 1983, proposed a merit pay system for master teachers as part of a solution to recognize quality in instruction. His proposal does not directly confront the problem of the poor to incompetent persons who are well ingrained into the educational system and often well protected.

Faculty tenure systems, while not originally intended to do so, have added much protection to the poor and incompetent instructors in education. Much of this protection is heightened by faculty unions which have been quick to defend their members against any administrative action intended to improve them or to dismiss them. The American Federation of Teachers (AFT) President, Albert Shanker, in an interview late in 1983 admitted that the AFT may need to look for ways to assist in the policing and getting bad teachers out of education:

> I admit that in the past we didn't play a role in policing our profession and I think now that that was a mistake. This is a reversal on my part. I've always felt that the union was the teacher's lawyer, and our job was to defend teachers when administrators try to remove them. (Gallagher, 1983, p. 17)

Both Shanker and Mary Fatrell, National Education Association (NEA) President, agreed that their organizations "must adopt higher profiles on the question of incompetent teachers." Fatrell estimated that up to 10 percent of the teachers may not be performing at acceptable levels.

Mr. Shanker went on to say that in the past he thought management was supposed to do the policing:

> I thought the business of policing was just a management function. But I think we're going to move in that direction, now. In the next year you'll find teachers doing more and more to play a role in getting bad teachers out of the classroom. (Gallagher, 1983, p. 24)

These statements should be warmly received by administrators and governing boards in the schools.

It would be easy to grab onto these statements and say, "See, this is the reason that we have allowed incompetent faculty to continue . . . the unions raised too much of a protest and the costs of fighting them are much too high . . ." This, however, is far from the total problem. To blame faculty and their unions for administrative and board of trustee neglect in policing and correcting abuses in the classroom is highly unfair. Many administrators have found procrastination a much easier route to follow than hard-nosed faculty evaluation.

In their review of the state of the art of teaching in two-year colleges, Cohen and Brawer (1977) spoke about the lack of effective evaluation systems in existence. They mentioned the efforts by many states in the early 1970s to mandate faculty accountability:

> Under the prodding of legislatures and state and local governing boards, administrators and instructors were to develop ways of assisting instructors to become accountable for their activities. Should an instructor be assessed and found wanting, he was to be assisted to improve, or failing that, to be severed from the institution. (p. 3)

They went on to say that "faculty evaluation remains of little effect." They pointed out how, as faculty took their cases into court, they usually won on such issues as due process, lack of effort by institutions to show they had taken efforts to "upgrade his skills," or because they were unable to prove persons were lacking or deficient in an "essential teaching area." They concluded that faculty dismissal continued to be very difficult and the burden of proof, which was difficult to properly document, remained with the institution (p. 3).

Evaluating for excellence in instruction actually begins for an educational institution when it starts accepting applications for a teaching or academic support position. Listing of the "preferred" academic and/or experience lets the potential candidate for a position know the level of background the college is looking for. Listing of the minimum acceptable qualifications level will help determine which group of candidates will apply.

Selecting candidates for positions should be done by an institution only after it has developed a profile or *"strawperson"* with the strengths and personality factors that will best fill the position. A combination of administrators and faculty members should agree to the strawperson profile and be involved in the interview process.

The careful screening and selection of faculty or academic support persons can eliminate many of the problems that otherwise may occur later. The second stage of evaluation begins as the person begins to phase into the position and assumes the total responsibilities outlined for the position.

Blee (1983) points out that the same process of evaluation for staff (non-teaching) begins with the initial selection of persons for appointment and "culminates with decisions concerning the retention or dismissal of personnel" (p. 68).

Research suggests that successful classroom management and organization by teachers "may be the primary enabling conditions of effective teaching" according to Evertson and Holley (1981, p. 108).

In dealing with the apprehension and fears that evolve in faculty evaluation, Bevan (1980) points out that "more than likely, it is the absence in the academic setting of a process regularly scheduled, systematically defined, seriously pursued, and appropriately reinforced that leads to feelings of apprehension" (p. 3).

DEFINING "EFFECTIVE CHARACTERISTICS" OF TEACHERS"

The definition of what effective teacher characteristics are is very illusive in the literature. There are a number of student evaluation of instructor forms that identify some areas of a job performance expected of faculty members in the classroom. The City Colleges of Chicago, Illinois, posed several questions to 30 "exemplary" teachers to find out what were the effective characteristics of these teachers (Guskey and Easton, 1983, p. 3-4). The results of their study is outlined as follows:

1. All of them were highly organized, planned carefully, had unambiguous objectives and high expectations for their students. Each class had a clear design:
   (a) an introduction at the beginning;
   (b) a summary at the end; and
   (c) a clear sequence of development in between.

2. All of them emphasized the importance of expressing positive regard for their students:
   (a) Most used some time during their first class session to become familiar with their students and contin-

ued to exchange personal information throughout the semester.

(b) They generally learned their students' names very early in the semester and addressed them by name.

3. They had an emphasis on encouraging student participation:

(a) They consistently asked questions during class to stimulate involvement.

(b) They also monitored student participation at frequent intervals to gain information as to whether the class was going well or if a change was needed.

4. In addition, they strongly emphasized the importance of providing students with regular feedback on their learning and rewarding learning successes.

(a) Feedback was generally provided through written comments on tests or papers.

(b) They frequently asked their students to see them after class to discuss learning problems.

(c) Written comments were also used to praise students' efforts and to make special note of improvements.

Reich (1983, p. 36) in explaining her excitement about why she continues to enjoy teaching says "I teach with students." She goes on to say that "although I am still concerned with content, I also see that if students don't understand it, I am getting through the material only for my benefit." She also sees the most exciting phase in teaching as being "the gap between what the teacher teaches and what the student learns . . . that is where the unpredictable transformation takes place, the transformation that means we are human beings, creating and defining our own world, and not objects, passive and defined." Reich projects a humanistic element into the core of her teaching which makes teaching for her "the practice of what it means to be human."

In describing the full-time faculty evaluation system at North County Community College, Poole and Dellow (1983) use the following indices as measures of teacher effectiveness:

1. Motivating students toward superior achievement within his or her courses;

2. Generating an enthusiasm in and establishing rapport with students;

3. Presenting material in an orderly and preplanned method compatible with the stated objectives of the course. The level and intensity of the instruction should be compatible with course and curriculum objectives;

4. Making maximum use of library resources, audiovisual aids, laboratory equipment, and so on;

5. Using a variety of teaching techniques to achieve the desired objectives;

6. Evaluating student performance adequately and equitably within the framework of the defined grading policy of the college;

7. Keeping course materials, including textbook selection and reference reading lists, up to date;

8. Providing sufficient time to assist students on an individual basis and encouraging students to take advantage of such assistance;

9. Providing instruction in such a way that it is effective to the greatest possible number of people.

There are some peer evaluation sample forms that have been developed to assess what have been determined to be criteria for good instruction in the classroom. Centra (1979) has presented a "Faculty Colleague Evaluation Questionnaire" that allows peers to evaluate those criteria that go beyond the classroom in university overall job evaluation. The questionnaire reviews such items as (1) research activity and recognition, (2) intellectual breadth, (3) participation in the academic community, (4) associated professional activities, and (5) public service or consulting. While this book is not presenting a case for self, peer, or student evaluations, there are certain elements in all of the tools used in these systems that are supposed to point to superior teaching if checked at the highest response levels on the forms.

TEACHING FORMATS

Wilkinson (1982) outlines the various types of teaching formats that take place. He suggests the three principal ones as the lecture, the laboratory session or field trip and the discussion class. In describing the lecture, he points to the amount of material that can be conveyed "efficiently and memorably to a large number of listerners," as one of its major attributes. Logical order and careful placement of material are seen as offering students a model on how to subdivide material and arrange it intelligibly. Wilkinson also feels that a lecturer can create excitement, curiosity, and appreciation for an area of specialized concern if he or she "conveys a spirit of excitement" (p. 4).

He points out that some small classes might be taught through discussion only. The greatest risk in such a format can be a lack of structure and organization. If discussion is able to lead into "meandering conversation full of intriguing tangents and autobiographical asides," he says it can "cease to lead to anywhere at all" (p. 7).

How effective any of the three teaching formats are for students is entirely dependent upon who is involved in the delivery of any one of the formats. It is here that some type of evaluation can help determine the degree of effectiveness. Centra (1979) points out that very little improvement can be expected by occasional observations by either colleagues or administrators if they "do not know what to look for or who may not be particularly effective teachers themselves" (p. 84).

In his review of the importance of the first class meeting between instructors and students, Wolcowitz (1982) points to several key points of significance for students:

1. It fulfills the obligation to tell students what to expect in the course (content and mechanics).

2. It also sets the atmosphere for the entire term.

3. The "student-teacher contract" comes out in the opening session in either the written course syllabus and/or in statements by the instructor.

Wolcowitz suggests that effective teaching "requires recognizing that the class is composed of individuals, each arriving with a different background and a different set of goals" (p. 11).
Other first class points of significance outlined are that:

4. The instructor should tell the students as specifically as possible what material will be covered in the course and why.

5. A well-constructed syllabus that outlines the major and minor subdivisions serves as a framework for students to organize their thoughts about the course.

6. The instructor should try to convey enthusiasm about the course material, as well as provide information.

7. The workload: students need to assess the amount of time involved for a course (length of the reading list; number and timing of exams and papers; how grades will be computed).

8. Students also want to know how to prepare for class and whether they should come to class if they are not prepared.

9. The standard operating procedures of the class should be established (time class begins; acceptability of asking questions; amount of time to be devoted to lecture, discussion; etc.).

Wolcowitz summarizes these issues by showing that the thing they all have in common is the role each one plays in "defining the atmosphere that the instructor would like to create in the classroom" (pp. 11-14).

How important is it for an instructor to know his or her students? Wolcowitz suggests that at "the most basic level, instructors should learn the names of their students." He says that "students generally work harder and respond in a more positive way if they believe the instructor views them as individuals rather than anonymous faces in a crowd" (p. 19).

Some of the items of information he feels are basic to knowing students that should be collected early are as follows (p. 20):

1. The student's year in college.
2. The student's field of concentration.
3. Other courses taken in the field and in related fields.
4. Other courses the student is taking that term.
5. Job experience.
6. Why the student is taking the course.

He also suggests a "preliminary written exercise" as another data gathering device. This description of the need to know the students coming to an instructor's classes was also highlighted earlier under point 2 by the "exemplary" teachers in the Chicago system who, as a group, emphasized "the importance of expressing positive regard for their students" (p. 3).

It would appear that no matter what teaching format is used, lecture, discussion, or laboratory, a much higher degree of success is expected with faculty knowing their students early and utilizing such knowledge in future interchanges throughout the semester or term.

Evertson and Holley (1981) point to some of the dynamics that can be *observed* in the classroom and are not available from any other source: classroom climate, rapport, interaction, and functioning of the classroom (p. 90).

THE ROLE OF FACULTY CLASSROOM ORGANIZATION

An administrative evaluation system needs to consider the various instructional components that can be assessed. The above material suggests that a quality hiring process precedes all other aspects of faculty evaluation. The type of class format, important aspects of the initial class, and knowledge of the students are all observable behaviors that can be evaluated by administrative evaluators. The organization of the material to be presented in a course is another vital aspect in the description of the strawperson of excellent instruction.

Diamond, Sharp, and Ory (1978) in the development of an "observational guide" for peer or colleague evaluation list the following points in relation to organization of the content and the instructor's clarity of presentation:

Organization of the Content

Logical sequence of topics

Pace of the lecture, discussion topics

Provision of summaries and synthesis

Appropriate use of class time

Instructor's Clarity of Presentation

Definition of new terms, concepts, and principles

Relevance of examples

Relationship to lab and discussion group assignments

The same authors have developed a rating scale for either self-evaluation or peer evaluation relative to the important aspects of a classroom presentation. The following is taken from the rating scale in the area of organization of content:

Introductory Portion

1. Stated the purpose of the lecture.

2. Presented a brief overview of the lecture content.

3. Stated a problem to be solved or discussed during the lecture.

4. Made explicit the relationship between today's and the previous lecture.

Body of Lecture

5. Arranged and discussed the content in a systematic

and organized fashion that was made explicit to the students.

6. Asked questions periodically to determine whether too much or too little information was being presented.

7. Presented information at an appropriate level of "abstractness."

8. Presented examples to clarify very abstract and difficult ideas.

9. Explicitly stated the relationships among various ideas in the lecture.

10. Periodically summarized the most important ideas in the lecture.

Conclusion of Lecture

11. Summarized the main ideas in the lecture.

12. Solved or otherwise dealt with any problems deliberately raised during the lecture.

13. Related the day's lecture to upcoming presentations.

14. Restated what students were expected to gain from the lecture material.

The introduction, body, and conclusion of a lecture or other type of class points to a very definite and organized approach to the presentation of the material. It calls for pre-classroom work on the part of the instructor. It also shows a "forward movement" which reviews the past presentation and transcends into what is expected next in an upcoming lecture.

Dubrow and Wilkinson (1982) point to the need to "chart your itinerary." They quote Gilbert Highet who had written that "the lecturer must know exactly what points he wishes to tell his audience, in what order, and with what emphasis." They suggest that "all but the most experienced and most accomplished lecturer must come equipped with notes; a detailed outline, with the major points and transitions between them set out legibly, is all that is really required" (p. 29).

TESTING EXPECTATIONS

It was stated earlier that an instructor should make known his or her number and timing of exams and the coverage each one will have. These should be included in the instructor's syllabus which is passed out the first day of class. Dubrow and Wilkinson suggest that students are generally pleased to have review sessions shortly before exams are given. They also appreciate a general description of the types of questions, how many, etc., that will be on the exam.

Nash (1982) puts the focus of the student in the fore-front in relationship to both the teaching process in total and the testing process more specifically:

> A class, in which the professor lectures for the entire semester and evaluates student performance at the end through a paper and exam, holds the student's academic role in suspense for rather a long period of time, and offers almost no acknowledgement of the student in the class-room. Hence if the student's learning evolves, only the student knows this. (p. 79)

He also states that "at its worst, it uncovers problems only after it is too late to correct them" (p. 79).

In his discussion on grading and evaluation, Jedrey (1982) emphasizes that the material to be tested on is to be "clearly delineated for the students." He goes on to suggest that students can only prepare properly for an examination if they know if it is to be a comprehensive one or will only include new material since the last exam.

In correcting exams, Jedrey says "you should at least point out major errors of fact and reasoning, note good points, and provide a coherent assessment at the end. The comments should praise and encourage as well as criticize, and should make clear the reason for the grade" (p. 110).

Baker (1983) points out the importance of feedback to students who are moving toward a goal.

THE USE OF QUESTIONING

Kasulis (1982) says that "skillful discussion leaders use questioning in such a way that they seldom have to lecture; they become part of the medium of the discussion" (p. 48). Not all faculty will achieve this level of skill but there are some guides that should improve questioning as a technique in the classroom for most faculty. The first is to see their students as individuals as mentioned above.

Kasulis says that such a focus will allow the faculty member to call on students at appropriate times, that is, "at the interesting moment when the individual's perspective would be the most relevant to the progress of the discussion" (p. 41).

In returning to Diamond, Sharp, and Ory's (1978) "self review" guide, the following items are listed to aid in evaluating good questioning techniques in a classroom:

Questioning Ability

1. Asked questions to see what the students knew about the lecture topic.

2. Addressed questions to individual students as well as to the group at large.

3. Used rhetorical questions to gain student's attention.

4. Paused after all questions to allow students time to think of an answer.

5. Encouraged students to answer difficult questions by providing cues or rephrasing.

6. When necessary, asked students to clarify their questions.

7. Asked probing questions if a student's answer was incomplete or superficial.

8. Repeated answers when necessary so the entire class could hear.

9. Received student questions politely and when possible enthusiastically.

10. Refrained from answering questions when unsure of a correct response.

11. Requested that very difficult, time-consuming questions of limited interest be discussed before or after class or during office hours.

The above items taken from the self-evaluation check list can also be used by administrative evaluators when evaluating a classroom presentation that calls for questioning.

SUMMARY

Developing a "strawperson" as a guide to effective evaluation of instruction by administrators is a must. Without such a guide, evaluation takes on a random, unstructured, ineffective look. The "strawperson" which the author attempted to pull together in this chapter provides a summary of some of the qualities and attributes usually given to excellent instructors. The chapter has not been designed to point the reader to one set of criteria for excellence in instruction, but rather to point out that there are many places that quality factors for instructors can be found. The Harvard-Danforth Center for Teaching and Learning and the Center for Improvement of Teaching and Learning of the City Colleges of Chicago are two such sources.

Both student and peer evaluation tools can be reviewed to find those characteristics that have been used to find the strongest traits that teachers have. Some of these forms have been well developed by university research personnel in the field of faculty evaluation. They can give an administrative evaluation program some very effective check points to use in classroom evaluations.

Administrators must enter the field of faculty evaluation open minded. While they may have been very effective faculty members utilizing specific teaching methodologies, they must develop an objectivity to other methods. Only by developing such an objectivity will they be able to properly assess other teaching methodologies used successfully by other faculty.

There are many things in a "strawperson" profile that are fairly easily observed and can be readily be evaluated by administrators. The course syllabus, scheduling of tests, day-to-day objectives, use of audio-visual support materials, promptness in starting class, are but a few. The evaluating of one's organization may present some more difficult problems if an instructor is evaluated only on a very limited basis as may be the case with tenured faculty. The individual class visit does have several points that can be used to raise organizational questions. The statement of objectives for a class period, review of previous material, student note-taking (or lack of it), questioning of students, and summary and prognosis for the next class are all indicators of the quality of preparation an instructor may have.

An administrative evaluation, made of a review for an upcoming exam or a review of such an exam after it is returned, will provide the evaluator data relevant to good testing, feedback, and grading techniques of the instructor. The degree of student involvement, use of student names (and other personal data), will also be available for evaluation purposes. Enthusiasm for the subject and teaching can also be observed.

While the area of course content may be one of the most troublesome for an administrative team to evaluate because of the limitations of their own academic backgrounds, such limitations should not be a deterrent. There are times a master teacher in a subject area may be asked to enter the classroom with an administrator and focus his or her attention on the accuracy of course content, choice of explanation, etc. A course syllabus may assist the evaluator to determine if the subject being presented is in line with the instructor's and/or department's course outline for the semester or term. A master teacher peer may also be asked to review exam content for comprehensiveness and appropriateness.

The non-classroom aspects of the faculty member's job also need to become a part of the "strawperson" profile. Faculty committees, selection of textbooks, work with advisory committees, providing of timely reports, and ability to get along with peers and administrators are all considerations in non-classroom evaluation.

Once faculty, administrators, and governing boards agree on a "strawperson" for their own institution, movement into an administrative evaluation format can evolve. The strawperson profile should be one that applies to faculty who are both tenured or non-tenured, and full or part-time.

2

"Faculty bargaining units leaned considerably more in the direction of protecting their members than toward enhancing professional performance."
—Cohen and Brawer, 1982

"Negotiating" and "Modeling" Away Board Responsibilities To Evaluate

THE ART OF FACULTY EVALUATION in community colleges appears to be no art at all. Cohen and Brawer (1982 p. 7) point out how, as faculty gained more power as they broke off from the lower schools, they made evaluation plans more complex.

Community college and high school faculty started bringing in the model of peer evaluation from their colleagues in the four-year colleges and universities. In addition, many of them added student evaluation to the process.

According to Anderson (1984), the halfway mark in the number of colleges in the United States having collective bargaining was reached when the California faculty voted for collective bargaining. She points out that "one significant outcome of this trend has been the gradual shift of certain areas of responsibility and authority (i.e. power) away from the traditional faculty committees and senates to the *line* organization of administrators (p. 20)." On the other hand, she refers to "lifeblood" decisions on retention, tenure, and promotion also being shifted away from the structure of a peer review committee made up of colleagues. This would be especially true in the more traditional four-year colleges and universities where peer evaluation had been used in most major personnel decisions. In Foleno v. Board of Education of the Township of Bedminster (Piele, 1979) the court went on to say "The board has the duty, in furnishing a thorough and efficient education, to evaluate the performances of its employees and to staff its classrooms with skillful and effective teachers" (p. 11).

In another case (Piele, 1979), the court was emphatic in its stand on *not negotiating evaluative criteria* into a contract (p. 147):

> Nevertheless, negotiation of evaluative criteria is against public policy because *retention or promotion of teachers is a management prerogative* [emphasis added].[1]

The laws in many states do not allow boards to delegate "discretionary authority" such as are found in the hiring or firing of teachers or other employees. Piele (1981, pp. 7-8) points out that " it is settled by law in most states that only the board hires and only the board fires.

There is much debate on what is negotiable into contractualized agreements between the board and the faculty union. Orze (1977, pp. 507-508) points out that "contractualized faculty power is not limitless," but have some boundaries which are clearly defined by legislative acts in those states which have made provisions for collective bargaining. He also points out that terms or conditions of employment "are ambiguous" and that little agreement is reached between unionized faculties and between states on what constitutes terms or conditions of employment which should (or must) be negotiated. Orze goes on to point out that the "legal powers of the union extend only to the mandatory subjects for collective bargaining that the administration must negotiate with it." He points out how a union is limited by its legal rights and/or by what management is willing to negotiate away beyond its need to negotiate:

> The union has no legal right to bargain for authority
> beyond these mandatory subjects. Whatever additional
> powers the union may gain at the bargaining table can
> only be achieved if the administration is willing to share
> one or more of its managerial rights with the union. The
> administration controls the scope of negotiations, and,
> in so doing, it determines the actual limits of the legal
> powers of the union. *Unions will attempt to expand the*
> *scope of bargaining as broadly as employers will allow them*
> *to* [emphasis added], but the employer always has the
> right to say no to any nonmandatory demand for negotia-
> tions. (pp. 507-508).

Orze goes on to point out that boards and administrators should be aware that once a subject is negotiated
into a contract, the employer will find it almost impossible to negotiate it back out if the union should insist
upon trying to retain it.

Some courts have disagreed with the New Jersey court's
stance on negotiation of evaluative criteria as being against
public policy (presented above). The North Dakota Supreme Court included teacher evaluation policies to be
permissive in negotiations.[2] The Indiana Supreme Court
was even more emphatic (Piele, 1981 p. 13). It stated
that teacher evaluation plans so "significantly touch and
concern the everyday activities of school teachers" that
the subject is within the "ordinary understanding" of the
term "working conditions" and, therefore, mandatorily
negotiable.[3] The appellate court had held that the school
board should have held prior discussion before it implemented a new teacher evaluation plan. The school board
had tried to work around the union by appointing a committee of non-union members. The appellate court referred
to evaluation as a "discussable" matter within the plain
and ordinary meaning of working condition.[4]

Whether a faculty evaluation system is left entirely
as a management prerogative, is "discussable" with the
union, or is negotiable as a working condition, much care
must be taken to assure that it accomplishes its goals.
It must assist faculty members to improve for retention
or promotional purposes and also must provide *assurances*

that incompetent faculty can be removed for the best
interests of students and public policy.

NEGOTIATING EVALUATIVE CRITERIA

It was outlined in Chapter 1 that a board of trustees
or board of education retains the right to hire and to fire
unless it is in conflict with a statute or a negotiated agreement.[5] In the "Collective Agreement" between the Faculty
Union/Ontario Council of Regents contract (1982-1984),
management's exclusive functions include:

> Hire, discharge, transfer, classify, assign, appoint, pro-
> mote, demote, lay-off, recall and suspend or otherwise dis-
> cipline employees subject to the right to lodge a grievance
> in the manner and to the extent provided in this agreement.
> (p. 12)

The "Agreement" between the Los Angeles Community
College District and its local AFT calls for regular employ-
no provisions for tenured faculty evaluation. It does,
however, spell out an evaluation procedure for non-tenured
faculty members (p. 14).

The "Agreement" between the Los Angeles Community
College District and its local AFT calls for regualr employees (those who have completed probationary status) to
be evaluated at least once every two academic years.
Their procedures include: (1) peer evaluation, which
uses student evaluations as part of its review process;
and (2) administrative evaluation.

The College of DuPage has not had a collective bargaining process in developing its procedures for evaluation.
In its procedures on tenured faculty development, a faculty
member's written statement (self-evaluation) and a student
rating questionnaire provide the major sources of information to be used in the formal evaluation conference.
DuPage's non-tenured evaluation procedures require both
student and self-evaluation but make classroom visitations
optional.

Carl Sandburg College in Illinois uses a four-part, non-tenured faculty evaluation system. It doesn't spell out the weight to be given to the four main input factors of: (1) peer evaluation, (2) student evaluation, (3) faculty professional report, and (4) supervisory evaluation. Their flow chart would indicate that each of the four factors carry an equal weight (Carl Sandburg College, p. 9).

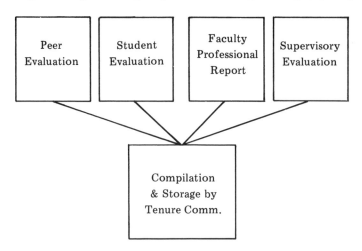

The University of Florida has sponsored a three-year National Faculty Evaluation Project for Community and Junior Colleges to assist eight community colleges to develop stronger faculty evaluation systems (Smith, 1983). The following is a summary of some of the elements which have been included in several of the evaluation systems that have been set up as a result of the UF project (pp. 9-15):

1. Arapahoe Community College (Littleton, CO)
   a. Annual self-evaluation
   b. Annual student evaluations of teaching faculty
   c. Peer evaluation every third year

2. Gateway Technical Institute (Racine, WI)
   The instructors formally evaluated in this system will have three evaluations (minimum):
   a. One by the instructor's coordinator
   b. Two others to be selected from student evaluations, self-evaluation, or a supervisor's evaluation.

3. Patrick Henry Community College (Martinsville, VA)
The following is a numerical/percentage breakout on Patrick Henry Community College's evaluation component of "teaching performance" which carries a weight of 70% in the overall evaluation process:

Min	Component	Student	Self	Supervisor
70%	1. Teaching Performance, or	65%	35%	0%
	2. Teaching, including classroom observation.	40%	30%	30%

This system works from the premise that all personnel holding faculty rank are presumed to possess the necessary professional qualifications to perform satisfactory in their positions, and that a "satisfactory" is expected of all faculty.

Smith (1983, pp. 14-15) points out that the faculty members under this system have the *option* of including classroom evaluation data from the supervisor in the evaluation plan but "most of the colleges in the University of Florida project . . . have placed less emphasis on classroom observations as a form of faculty evaluation." He suggests that the trend away from classroom visitations may be due to the research by Centra (1979) which supposedly was found to be highly unreliable.

RESPONSE TO THE NATIONAL FACULTY EVALUATION PROJECT

The University of Florida National Faculty Evaluation Project needs and demands some attention and critical response. This project comes at a time when the national emphasis is on quality in the classroom and much emphasis is being placed on getting the "deadwood" out of the classroom. Smith and his colleagues appear to have taken the *ineffective* system of faculty evaluation present as the model in many four-year colleges and universities and transported it into a number of two-year colleges as a "conceptual framework model."

An analysis of each of the above models introduced in the individual community college finds the heavy emphasis on evaluation to be coming from student evaluation, self-evaluation, and peer review. The administrative evaluation percentage in any of Smith's project colleges ranges from a high of 25-30 percent down to 0 percent! How do these colleges justify such an evaluation system as having any accountability to their public and their boards of trustees?

Smith has sidestepped the above issue by his statement that "the trend away from classroom visitations may be due to the research by Centra (1979), which shows this form of teaching evaluation to be highly unreliable." A thorough review of Centra's work would indicate that he did not devote *any* of his chapters to research on administrative evaluation. Centra indicated early in his book that his emphasis would be on research studies in student ratings, colleague input, and self-evaluations (p. 3). Most of the research presented by Centra also came out of the universities.

Centra, while presenting the research on student, peer, and self-evaluation, w*as not* especially supportive of any of the three methods. The following are summary comments found on these three evaluation systems.

On Student Evaluations:

1. The correlation between grades and ratings (student) is usually in the .20 range (p. 32).

2. The manipulation of ratings by teachers must be considered when ratings are used for personnel decisions (p. 44).

3. The teacher who is lenient in assigning grades and out-of-class work is not improving learning, yet may be better rated by some students (p. 45).

4. Because of the positive bias in student ratings, teachers who need to improve may not realize their weaknesses.

On Self Evaluation:

1. In a study of 343 teaching faculty, teachers self-ratings had only a modest relationship with student

ratings—a median correlation of .21.

2. For many teachers who have an inflated view of their performance, a view that might become even more inflated or defensive if their assessments were used administratively, self-evaluations are of little use in making tenure, promotion, and salary decisions (p. 48).

On Colleague Ratings:

1. In these studies, faculty members did not visit each other's classes systematically, if at all (p. 74).

2. The first finding was that colleagues were generous in their ratings (p. 74).

3. On the item "evaluating overall instructor effectiveness," 94 percent were either "excellent" or "good;" student ratings were also favorable, but not to the same extent as colleagues' ratings (p. 74).

4. A second finding showed colleague ratings to be not statistically reliable; the average correlation among ratings by different colleagues was about .26 for each item. This low reliability *casts doubt on the value of colleague ratings* [emphasis added] as they were collected in this study (p. 75).

Centra goes on to say that one possiblity for improving faculty colleague evaluation reliability is to "train" faculty on good observation techniques, "since trained observers make sounder judgments than untrained observers' (p. 76). This last point is similar to the one being made by this author relative to the development of reliable administrative evaluation systems. None of the research studies presented by Centra appear to justify the development of "model" evaluation systems that utilizes student, self, and peer reviews but that comes close to totally rejecting any administrative *evaluation of instruction* responsibility. During the 1983 national conference of the American Association of Community and Junior Colleges (AACJC) in New Orleans, the National Faculty Evaluation Project people presented a roundtable discussion on their project to date. This author was present and asked the question "How many faculty have been fired in the eight colleges in the project over its first three years?" The reply was "None [0] to date!" A thorough review of the last thirteen years of *The Yearbook of School Law* (1972 through 1983) did not locate one case where a student, peer, or self-evaluation system led to dismissal of a faculty member. On the other hand, numerous cases were found where administrative evaluation and dismissals were supported by the courts. The following are statements abstracted from four faculty dismissal cases which are presented in Chapter 7 in summary form (and with appropriate references):

1. In *Chung v. Park* a tenured professor was dismissed. . . especially because of poor teaching supported by substantial evidence.

2. In *Whaley v. Anoka-Hennepin Independent School District* the court found substantial evidence which supported four major teaching deficiencies. Six classroom observations were undertaken over a five-month period.

3. In *Hickey v. Board of Directors of Pennsylvania Manor School* seven unsatisfactory classroom evaluations leading to dismissal were upheld by the court.

STATEWIDE BARGAINING

The State of Pennsylvania placed the Public Employee Relations Act of Pennsylvania (ACT 195) into effect October 21, 1970. It paved the way for statewide negotiations between the commonwealth and the 4,500 faculty members of Pennsylvania's thirteen state colleges. Procedures that were negotiated for tenured faculty included the following according to Hornbeck (1977):

> Tenured faculty members are evaluated every five years or more often if necessary. A primary basis for the evaluation is a written statement by the faculty member covering the four areas of professional growth and development,

intellectual growth and development, college service, and community services. In each instance the statement will reflect on the previous five years and will suggest areas for change and improvement. A system is also laid out by which student evaluation will play a role. (p. 450)

One of the assumptions the Pennsylvania system works under is that every faculty member can show improvement regardless of how good they are.

A second statewide bargaining agreement to be reviewed here is one between the Massachusetts Board of Regents of Higher Education for the Massachusetts Regional Community College Council and the Massachusetts Teachers Association (affiliate of the National Education Association, NEA). The procedure section (pp. 13-4) spells out five processes for evaluating faculty and weights for each one:

1. Student evaluation (30%)
2. Course materials evaluation (25%)
3. Classroom observation evaluation (25%)
4. Student advisement & college service evaluation (20%)
5. Summary evaluation

The student evaluation appears to have been organized as a key part of the Massachusetts system while administrative evaluation is severely limited.

FROM CONTRACT TO GRIEVANCE . . .

The use of collective bargaining agreements to set up grievance procedures for faculty members is very common and allowable under the scope of bargaining. Grievable items are limited to contractual clauses in contracts relative to wages, hours, and working conditions. Since the mandatory scope of bargaining has limitations due to "management rights" provisions, state statutes, and/or by interpretations made by the courts and board or management's inherent rights, the decisions by the various states are not greatly disparate according to Piele (1979, pp. 144-145).

Piele points out that once procedures are negotiated into a contract, it does *not negate* a management's rights (p. 163). Such might well be the case of management's exclusive right to hire and to fire personnel. In order to properly assess or evaluate the work of personnel, management may wish to negotiate evaluation procedures into a collective bargaining agreement. Whether such procedures include administrative,- student,- peer- or self-evaluation procedures is open to negotiation in some states. The Michigan Supreme Court in 1978 ruled that "adoption of student evaluations of faculty was within the mandatory scope of bargaining since it would affect reappointment, tenure, and promotion" (Piele, 1979, p. 146).[7] A case supporting a management rights clause was decided by the Kentucky Court of Appeals. It held that a decision to not re-employ two non-tenured faculty was *not* grievable. It cited "the right of dismissal given to a board is absolute and can not be limited by contract" (Piele, 1978, p. 175).[8]

An Iowa school's negotiated contract clause was found by the the Iowa Supreme Court to be contrary to public policy. The Davenport Community School District had allowed its negotiated grievance procedure to include possible arbitration of faculty members' non-renewal of their contract. The Supreme Court ruled the board *could not* negotiate away such responsiblity and give it to an arbitrator for a final decision on termination (Piele, 1979, p. 155).[9] Similar cases were decided in the states of New York and Florida in 1977 and 1978 respectively.

In the Collective Bargaining Agreement of Rio Hondo Community College District in California, the contract makes it very clear that *administrative evaluation* is the criteria system the board of trustees had selected. It has, however, been willing to allow those procedures for the evaluation system to be negotiated into its faculty contract. It has also provided a clause in the contract which states:

> The District accepts as a fundamental premise for a successful evaluation program the necessity for mutual respect and confidence to exist between the evaluator and those evaluated. To promote this respect and confidence the District will provide training for administrators in the process of evaluation.

The choice of the type of evaluation criteria to be used

appears to be one of the *inherent* and/or *implied rights* of board of trustees. The need to "discuss" such criteria and procedures with a faculty collective bargaining unit has received some court support in several states. How much input and how detailed the procedures become will depend in a large degree on how much of this authority boards wish to negotiate over to their faculty. Contracts which have negotiated away too much authority so as to be contrary to public policy and/or to restrict boards exclusive rights in hiring or firing of personnel have been negated by the courts.

FROM GRIEVANCE TO ARBITRATION . . .

The final step in some negotiated contract grievance clauses and procedures is arbitration. What can be arbitrated will depend on how broad the arbitration clause is in a contract. A very broad clause may allow for all aspects and clauses within the contract to be arbitrated. A New Jersey Superior Court used two major conditions to determine if an issue was arbitrable:

> (1) The subject of the dispute is a matter that is negotiable and not a matter of major educational policy within the school board's managerial prerogative, and (2) the dispute is covered by the negotiated arbitration provision of the contract. (Piele, 1979, p. 149)

When does a school have to go to arbitration? In Connecticut the Supreme Court has specifically pointed to a "positive assurance" test. In this test "judicial inquiry should be granted only when it may be said with *positive assurance* that the arbitration clause is not susceptible of an interpretation that covers the asserted dispute" (Piele, 1979, p. 148).

Piele (1977) summarizes the question on whether or not a case is arbitrable or should go to the courts as being a question answered by state law, the specific contract arbitration provision, and the subject matter being considered. An arbitrator's jurisdiction usually centers on procedural arbitrability (p. 259). The "essence test" or "common law test" is often applied by a court in reviewing an arbitrator's decision. The "essence test" is a test of the arbitrator's decision relative to a remedy that is (1) not prohibited, (2) is rationally connected to the breach of contract, and (3) is gounded in the "essence" of the contract (Piele, 1977, p. 262). The "essence" comes from an interpretation and application of the agreement.

In summary, arbitration may be a step in a contract grievance clause. In some states, arbitration is looked at as the means to resolve institutional disputes outside of the courts. In some states, arbitration is prescribed by statutes dealing with dismissal of tenured faculty.

SUMMARY

Collective bargaining is one way faculty have begun to negotiate evaluation systems. The courts have been fairly consistent in making it clear that *criteria* for faculty evaluation is a board of trustees prerogative and implied responsibility. They have also allowed boards to negotiate evaluation *procedures* into collective bargaining agreements. The form these evaluation systems take varies by state (in statewide negotiated contracts) and by individual college collective bargaining agreements. Cohen and Brawer (1982, p. 75) refer to evaluation procedures becoming more complex and gaining "labyrinthime complexity." In addition, there are many other "model" systems being set up. This chapter reviewed such a system being set up in eight colleges under the leadership of the University of Florida.

The complexity of a system such as the statewide system of Massachusetts makes it extremely difficult to find out if the goal of improving instruction is met. Student evaluations are given more weight than any other phase of their evaluation system which includes administrative in-class evaluation. The studies presented by Centra and others showed how *skewed* to the *positive side* were student evaluations of faculty members. Students are, as a group, very generous and unrealistic in their evaluations. In a system that gives more weight to unsophisticated student responses than it gives to its professional evaluators will, undoubtedly, fire very few incompetent faculty members. Solid administrative evaluation data documenting an instructor's incompetence in preparation, subject matter, organization, and classroom teaching techniques can be significantly compromised by an "average" evaluation in the student evaluation part of the total evaluation system. The Massachusetts evaluation system shows enough of an administrative compromise that it has, in fact, watered down the potential for improvement in instruction or dismissal of incompetent faculty that exists in a more heavily weighted administrative evaluation system.

Cohen and Brawer (1982, p. 75) pointed out that, while some contracts mandated evaluation procedures for all faculty in a given institution (or state system), "faculty bargaining units leaned considerably more in the direction of protecting their members than toward enhancing professional performance."

It will greatly enhance the cause of excellence in education if evaluation policies and procedures are reviewed and strengthened by Governing Boards and top-level administrators. Such a review must include putting a proper weight on the elements as well as limiting the type of elements to be included in evaluation. It should consider eliminating the impact that both student and peer evaluation have had on watering down a more valid evaluation system. The research on student, self, and peer evaluation show all three systems to be very weak and unreliable as deterrents to poor instruction. They have had the impact of perpetuating the incompetent and protecting those who are creating the damage to the total education process that has been documented in study after study in the mid-1980s.

The Pennsylvania system uses a "self evaluation" approach. Individual faculty members provide a written statement evaluating themselves over the previous five years. Such a system leaves itself wide open for criticism when so much of the evaluation weight is given to self appraisal. There are no cases documented of faculty self evaluations leading to a firing or dismissal from any educational institution.

Educational institutions are at the crossroads for determining if they are willing to bite the bullet on selecting effective evaluation criteria options. Will they continue to accept the easy option of student evaluations as a major criteria in their evaluation-of-faculty? The barrage of "new" student evaluation forms from commercial firms is almost overwhelming to top instructional administrators and/or division chairpersons. Each of these forms *promises* to get at the deeper student responses which will improve faculty instruction better than any of the other dozens of student evaluation forms in the market place. Centra's research on the psychology of student evaluation shows their responses to be "very generous" to faculty. Only 10-12 percent of students ever see an instructor as less than average in their eyes. If one believes empirical research such as that pulled together by Centra and others, it is hard to believe that any new, revised, or computer-scored student evaluation form will have any significant impact upon how students evaluate their instructors.

If educational governing boards sincerely accept their responsibilities in both the hiring, granting of tenure, and firing of faculty, they must *not* allow the process of contract negotiations to distract from their authorities by spelling out a faculty evaluation system aimed at protecting faculty to the detriment of improved instruction or the right to dismiss incompetent faculty. Those negotiated contracts which put major emphasis on student, peer, and/or self evaluation have put boards of trustees and administrators in just such a position. It is *time to avoid* any further"negotiating away" of board of trustee powers and responsibilities and to reverse such clauses in faculty contracts where they exist.

The improvement of instruction in education has to be of prime importance for the mid to late 1980s and beyond. Governing Boards are in a position to make sure that it reaches such a level of high importance!

CHAPTER 2 ENDNOTES

[1]Teacneck Bd. of Educ. v. Teaneck Teachers Ass'n, 390 A.2d 1198 (N.J. Super. 1978).

32   Evaluating for Excellence

[2] Fargo Educ. Ass'n. v. Fargo Pub. School Dist. No. 1, 291 N.W.
2d 267 (N.D. 1980).

[3] Evansville-Vanderburgh School Corp. v. Roberts, 405 N.E. 2d 895,
898-99 (Ind. 1980).

[4] Evansville-Vanderburgh School Corp. v. Roberts, 395 N.E. 2d 291
(Ind. Ct. App. 1979), reconsidering, 392 N.E. 2d 810 (Ind. Ct. App.
1979).

[5] Foleno v. Board of Educ. of the Twp. of Bedminster, Decision
of N.J. Comm'r of Educ. (1978).

[6] Central Michigan University Faculty Ass'n. v. Central Michigan
Univ., 273 N.W. 2d 21 (Mich. 1978).

[7] Brown and Holton Educ. Ass'n. v. Holton Publ. Schools, 258
N.W. 2d 51 (Mich., 1977) rev'g 254 N.W. 2d 41 (Mich. App. 1977).

[8] Moravek v. Davenport Comm. School Dist., 262 N.W. 2d 797
(Iowa, 1978).

3

*Qualifications state what one
should be able to do . . . competency
what one has proven to be able to do . . .*

—Andrews, 1984

Determining Qualifications and Competencies of Faculty

AMERICAN SECONDARY EDUCATION needs to take a critical look at its system of faculty qualifications. Problems in qualification levels for faculty are not usually seen as problems when new faculty are hired. Colleges and universities graduate teachers with majors of twenty-four to thirty or more credit hours within a degree. The defects in the secondary schools' qualification system start showing up during times of faculty retrenchment. During retrenchment "minimum" (state defined) qualification levels take over as does an outdated strict seniority system.

It is not unusual for a more senior faculty member to be moved into a new teaching subject area with a minimum of credit hours of course preparation in their college background. State education systems refer to these as *minimum qualifications* and they are often *legislated*. The term "minimum qualifications" should be a clear signal to both educators and non-educators that the quality of education will go through some severe losses during periods of faculty retrenchment when seniority is the main, and often only, criteria for retention in the school system.

The community college system in the United States has developed without legislated qualifications and competencies for faculty and other support personnel. This was documented in a recent national study of community college state systems throughout the United States (Andrews and Mackey, 1983, unpublished). Andrews and Mackey, in their study, found the following conditions to prevail in most states having a community college system:

1. Local boards of trustees still have control in the majority of community colleges in determining faculty and staff qualifications.

2. State agency guidelines usually suggest the master's degree for general studies/transfer subject areas and a minimum of a bachelor's degree in occupational and technical subject areas with one to three years of related job experience.

3. There were no *legally defined minimum qualifications* in any of the thirty-five states that responded to the survey.

This national study of community college qualifications for faculty did find a fairly common "recommended" qualifications level as summarized in point number two above. A total of twenty-two states mentioned specifically that the local community college boards are able to set the qualifications standards. The remaining thirteen states referred to one or more state boards for coordinating community colleges, a state board of regions, department of education or some other similar agency at the state level as providing "guidelines" for the minimum community college faculty qualifications.

An Illinois community college tenure law, which went into effect in January of 1980, specified that in considering seniority in faculty reductions, a faculty member would not be released if the person is "competent to render" a teaching service being offered by a less senior faculty member:

The problem such legislation presents in a community college system such as Illinois' and many other states is that "competent to render" has not been spelled out as to what it means in terms of qualifications and competencies of faculty members.

DEFINING MINIMUM QUALIFICATIONS AND COMPETENCIES FOR FACULTY

Several Illinois Community Colleges have attempted to determine some minimum qualification levels for faculty since the passage of the tenure law. William Rainey Harper College worked out a plan that was largely outlined by faculty members. It left any questionable areas of interpretation in the hands of departmental faculty members. Illinois Valley Community College developed what may be the most comprehensive analysis of minimum qualifications of any community college in the nation. It presents a detailed qualification level for each program of study, departmental, and individual courses. This analysis has been summarized into a *Qualifications Handbook*.

Community colleges have an opportunity to set the minimum acceptable levels at a high enough level so that they can avoid the tragic movement that has been taking place in secondary schools. Many secondary schools have been having reduction in force (R.I.F.) due to declining student enrollments. These schools usually have legislated minimum standards for teaching specific course areas. The standards are far from satisfactory for the complex and specialized educational needs of students in the latter part of the 20th century. It is not uncommon to find that two to six college credit hours are all that are needed to satisfy the legislated minimum standards for some specific course areas.

The reductions in force faced by many schools have led to persons teaching in fields and courses in which they have little to no interest, no experience, or no previous teaching time. There are no specified time-line limitations on when those minimum hours should have been earned. The faculty members with most seniority often end up teaching course areas with which they are

out of touch and are often starting with much obsoles-
cence and outdated background material. This movement
of "gerrymandering" secondary faculty members into
positions requiring new preparation with a minimum of
qualifications has come at a time when several national
studies have pointed out the need to upgrade the requirements for students in secondary schools. It is well past
time when state legislatures should review and strengthen
the college hours required for faculty to teach in all subject areas.

DEFINING QUALIFICATIONS AND COMPETENCIES— AN OPPORTUNITY

It would behoove each community college to consider
the issue and challenge of defining their own minimum
qualifications for faculty and other related positions
(assistants to instruction, librarians, and counselors) and
spell out how one can become "competent to render"
a teaching or related service. Qualifications should be
defined at a high enough level to reflect the "quality"
of teaching a community college should expect. This will
help significantly to eliminate the possibility of reducing
faculty strictly on the basis of seniority. Reduction,
primarily by seniority, is much more likely in the *absence*
of either legislated or board of trustee defined minimum
standards.

When board of trustees' policies are in place and an
established "catalog" of minimum qualifications are defined, the next step in developing a comprehensive evaluation system is to see how individual faculty and other
support staff fit into this system. Any established college
which moves to incorporate such a system will have to
deal with many of its faculty who have taught at the
institution for long periods of time.

In dealing with individual qualifications and competencies there has to be agreement on what the terms mean.
The following definitions will be used to define qualified,
competent, and competencies for the remainder of this
book:

1. *QUALIFIED*—This term will be used to designate the minimum preparation level necessary for teaching or academic support employees to be hired for a *specific area of instruction* or an academic support position.

2. *COMPETENT*—This term will be used to refer to a teaching or academic support employee who has both the minimum preparation level and who has successfully undergone the tenure evaluation system and/or has successfully prepared for and taught individual courses or performed satisfactorily in other job services.

3. *COMPETENCIES*—This term will be used to spell out exact areas of competence of a faculty member or academic support employee.

The term qualified refers to the initial and subsequent academic credentials a teacher or academic support person brings to a job when hired. In the case of occupational program faculty, such qualification can include the hours of preparation they bring from job experiences. It is important to note that, in the above definitions, it is not assumed that a person who is qualified for a job is also considered competent. Exhibit 1 presents a sample of how minimum qualifications might be defined for a business division in a community college.

Competency is earned by the person through proving his or her abilities in subject matter and teaching performance on the job. Competence is earned through the evaluation system of the college in which the person is working. Administrators throughout the United States and in the Canadian colleges and secondary schools will identify with the need to have a faculty or academic support person earn their reputation at the school in which they are working. Too many "qualified" persons have been shuffled between secondary schools and colleges with the assumption they are competent because of their credentials and letters of recommendation.

In the system that is being outlined in this book, competence in courses and other job responsibilities is developed during the two- or three-year non-tenured probationary period prior to the awarding of tenure. Tenure as awarded by boards of trustees or boards of education should be based upon solid evidence of "competence" coming out of a solid administrative evaluation system. Competenices as defined above should result in an exact listing of courses (or academic support services) in which a person has attained competence. Faculty members or academic support persons may continue to gain competence in additional courses or job services as they teach or perform in these new areas.

EXHIBIT 1

MINIMUM QUALIFICATIONS
TO TEACH VARIOUS SUBJECT AREAS IN
BUSINESS DIVISION

Transfer Courses

Approximately 25 percent of the courses taught in the division are transfer-articulated courses. They do, however, enroll close to 50 percent of the Business Division's total enrollments in such courses as Accounting and Computer science. The administration and faculty agree that the *Master's Degree* is the desired minimum *qualification needed* in the transfer-level courses in this division.

Occupational Programs

There are five occupational degree programs and eight certificate programs offered in the division. Generally the *Bachelor's Degree* is the desired minimum *qualification needed* in the various occupational disciplines of the Business Division.

Successful Teaching Experience

Successful teaching experience is preferred for persons in all of the teaching disciplines in this division. Successful work related experience is also required in the occupational programs. In hiring part-time faculty, the work experience might outweigh prior teaching experience in certain occupational programs.

EXHIBIT 1 (continued)

Subject Area Minimum Qualifications

ACCOUNTING (Transfer & Upper Level)—Master's degree in Accounting, Business Administration, Finance, or Business Education. Qualifications must include 30 hours of Accounting and Finance course work. Related business and/or teaching experience will be given consideration in lieu of hours requirement. Also, Bachelor's degree in Business plus C.P.A. or C.M.A. certificate is acceptable.

ACCOUNTING (Non-Transfer)—Bachelor's degree in Accounting, Business Administration, Finance, or Business Education. Qualifications must include 18 hours of Accounting; also, work experience in Accounting, Bookkeeping, Data Processing (minimum of 2,000 hours).

BUSINESS ADMINISTRATION (Transfer)—Master's degree in Business Administration, Business Education, M.S. in Business, Law Degree, Master's in Economics. Related business and/or teaching experience will be considered for individuals with Master's degree in area other than those listed above.

BUSINESS ADMINISTRATION (Non-Transfer)—Bachelor's degree in Business Administration, Business Education, Economics, to include 18 hours in area taught; also, work experience in area taught (minimum of 2,000 hours).

COMPUTER SCIENCE (Transfer)—Master's degree in Information Science/Computer Science or Master's degree in Mathematics or Business plus work experience in D.P./C.S.I. area. Qualifications to include 24 graduate hours of Data Processing/Information Science/Computer Science course work.

DATA PROCESSING (Non-Transfer)—Bachelor's degree in Business Mathematics or Computer Science. Qualifications to include 24 hours of Data Processing/Information Science/Computer Science course work; also, work experience in D.P./C.S.I. Information Science area (minimum of 2,000 hours).

The listing and maintaining of a faculty or academic support member's competencies becomes a management auditing function and should become an important part of a faculty member's personnel file. Individual competency forms can be developed to list the competencies each person has attained. The bottom half of the forms can spell out those qualifications that each person has reported, but that have not been tested in relation to the competency status of courses or services listed in the top half of the form. The qualifications are developed from academic transcripts and/or previous work experience.

The Individual competency forms should allow room for signatures of both the individual faculty or academic support person and of two administrative supervisory personnel. Signatures can give a "contractual" significance to both sides. They can offer protection to the faculty member if these is a turn-over in administrative personnel at the department, division, or dean's level. It also shows that agreement has been reached for the listing of both competencies and qualifications.

INITIAL DEFINING OF COMPETENCIES
AND QUALIFICATIONS

Administrators have a major task ahead of them the first time they move to identify the competencies and qualifications of each of their full-time faculty and academic support personnel. The process involves very close analysis of all transcripts in personnel folders. It also involves reviewing past records to determine teaching or other services which may have led to a competency status in the institution.

There will be disagreements as the process progresses. Some faculty members will wish to have competency in courses that they have taught over a period of time (sometimes several years) and may not have the academic qualifications to teach based upon the college's newly defined *Qualifications Handbook*. Others will insist on competency in courses they have never taught and/or in courses in other divisions of the college.

"GRANDFATHERING IN"
ESTABLISHED COMPETENCIES

The administration must make it clear that it will not compromise on all of the exceptions to the qualifications in their *Qualifications Handbook.* They should not attempt to "protect" all existing personnel who may not fit the qualifications being recommended as "minimal." The possibility of "grandfathering in" some competencies can provide the vehicle necessary to recognize previous successful teaching experiences or academic support services that would otherwise not be recognized in the minimum standards of the qualifications handbook (Andrews and Mackey, pp. 71-72).

It is important that administrators not "grandfather in" each and every course or service that has been taught or performed previously. If a person has not taken course work in a subject field for 15 to 25 years and has not kept professionally up-to-date in the subject area, grandfathering should be withheld. It is possible that competency can be placed in a "probationary" status with some activities spelled out to regain full competency status. Some suggestions are outlined below:

> *_____ has also taught Economics 208 and 209 for a number of years. With the new demands by transfer colleges on Economics student transfers, it is agreed that _____ needs to update her Economics background through coursework to continue teaching this course beyond the 1984-85 academic year.

Persons have sometimes "filled in" to teach a course they are not properly credentialed to teach because of staffing needs by a department at various times. It is easy to forget the *reason* for such an assignment and mislead a faculty member into thinking he or she is qualified strictly by having taught the course(s). The above concerns are raised to keep some integrity to the system. Students should be guaranteed they will be taught by persons who are properly qualified in their courses.

A close review of academic credentials may produce some areas in which a person has coursework equal in credit hours to the minimum qualifications level but with some very poor grades. In such a case, not listing as qualified certain courses because of grades would be in order, and again would add integrity to the process of providing a system of quality to a college.

MOVING FROM QUALIFIED TO COMPETENT

Colleges need to work out a system that allows a person to move from qualified status into competent status for courses or services that are initially listed in the "qualified" section of an individual's competency sheet. The following is a recommended procedure that will provide an orderly and meaningful recognition of new competencies for faculty:

Persons who have been deemed qualified to teach courses in their *own* division can ask their chairperson for the opportunity to teach one or more of these courses. The instructors will then properly prepare for, teach, and be evaluated in their efforts in the teaching of the course. The evaluation will consist of reviewing course outlines, articulation efforts by the instructor with other faculty/chairpersons who have taught the course, and some classroom visitation(s) by the administration. The process may be completed after one or two semesters of teaching the course. The instructor's individual competency sheet will be changed to add "new competencies" when the time arrives.

The process can be summarized into a check form (see Exhibit 3).

EXHIBIT 2

SUGGESTED PROCEDURE TO OBTAIN COMPETENCY STATUS

Procedure for
Full-Time Tenured Faculty Members
to Obtain Competency Status for a Course
on Their Individual Competency Evaluation Forms

Full-time faculty members at _____ Community College or Secondary School who wish to obtain competency status for a course within their division that they are *qualified for but have not previously taught* may follow the following procedure:

1. Talk to the Division Chairperson and make the request in writing to be considered for teaching of a course within the division that the faculty member has been deemed qualified to teach.

2. The Division Chairperson will make an effort to assign such a course if it is possible within the scheduling needs of students and the overall division members.

3. The faculty member(s) assigned to a new course preparation will properly prepare for the course and be administratively *evaluated* during the semester(s)/term(s) that the course is taught.

4. A determination of competency will be made prior to the end of the semester(s) or term(s) in which the course is taught. A second or third semester or term may be determined necessary for further evaluation before competency is granted.

MAINTAINING COMPETENCIES

One major item missing in most faculty competency systems is that of having a system of determining how a faculty or academic support person maintains the competencies they have. There should be a reasonable timeframe and some action expected in the maintenance of one's competencies. The following faculty questions relative to keeping or losing competencies are answered using a

EXHIBIT 3

FACULTY COMPETENCY ASSIGNMENT SHEET

NAME _____

DIVISION _____ Social Science

	DATE COMPETENCY GIVEN	DATE(S) TAUGHT PAST 5-YR. PERIOD													
		1977-78		1978-79		1979-80		1980-81		1981-82		1982-83		1983-84	
COMPETENCIES		FALL	SP	FALL	SP	FALL	SP	FALL	SP	FALL	SP	FALL	SP	FALL	SP
1. EDC 100	9/16/81			X											X
2. EDC 200	9/16/81		X											X	X
3. EDC 202	9/16/81	X	X		X	X	X	X	X	X	X	X	X	X	X
4. PSY 100	9/16/81	X				X	X	X	X	X	X	X	X	X	X
5. PSY 200	9/16/81												X		
6. PSY 201	9/16/81	X	X	X	X	X	X	X	X		X	X	X	X	X
7.															
8.															
9.															
10.															
11.															
12.															
QUALIFICATIONS															
1. HIS 100															
2. HIS 101															
3. HIS 200															
4. HIS 201															
5. SOC 100															
6.															
7.															
8.															

COMMENTS: _____

"five-year time period" providing the framework for maintaining competencies:

FACULTY QUESTION 1: Can competencies be withdrawn?

Yes. If an instructor/academic support person disregards keeping up-to-date in a subject/discipline area, and/or does not teach a course over a five-year period, and/or generally neglects keeping current in an area, competency very likely will be withdrawn.

FACULTY QUESTION 2: Does this mean an instructor has to teach *every course* on his/her competency list during a five-year period?

No. An instructor teaching a higher-level course in his/her field will not be expected to teach the lower-level course that provides the background necessary for the higher level course.

FACULTY QUESTION 3: How does one maintain the competencies that are initially agreed to?

Continued teaching of the subject is one way. Each course should be taught during any five-year period with the exception mentioned in the answer for question No. 2 above. However, continued effort to obtain coursework, articulation efforts, advisory committee work, attending workshops in the course(s), keeping up-to-date through journals, etc., all add to the "maintenance of competencies."

FACULTY QUESTION 4: Can faculty and academic support personnel become qualified in other areas by taking coursework and then move to become competent?

Yes, to the first part of the question. They can become qualified by the minimum qualifications that have been set up in the Governing Board's *Qualifications Handbook.*

No, to the second part of the question. The following Governing Board policy covers this:
"The establishment of competencies outside of a

person's present position will only affect such personnel in their academic year assignments, overloads, and summer sessions at such time as staff reduction(s) may affect their present status as a full-time employee. In such a case, the persons must make a formal request to their immediate supervisor to teach or perform the necessary assignments of the job in case of an academic support position. Supervisory evaluation will determine if competency is to be given."

COMPETENCIES AND STAFF REDUCTIONS

There is another major issue that underscores the development of a comprehensive institutional competency and qualifications faculty and academic support evaluation system. The question with faculty is, "How will individual competencies be used in staff reductions?" This question must be dealt with if the process is to have any meaning in establishing and maintaining *quality standards* for teaching and academic support staff. In keeping with the theme of the importance of administrative faculty evaluation for the improvement of instruction, the following is a logical response to the faculty question:

The term *competent* will carry much more weight than the term *qualified* in the school's posture to retain faculty in their present teaching or academic support *jobs*. The law (tenure) specifically uses the term "competent to render" but leaves it up to the schools to define. This school has defined *competent* as the term used to refer to a teaching or academic support employee who has both the minimum preparation level (qualifications) and who has successfully undergone the tenure evaluation system and/or has since successfully prepared for, taught, and been evaluated in additional individual courses.

SUMMARY

Defining key terms is undoubtedly one of the most important tasks a community college faces in the establishment of a faculty competency and qualification system aimed to fit each of its individual faculty and academic support personnel. This chapter has attempted to provide the reader with a proposal that establishes an active system of determining, maintaining, and managing individual and institutional competencies and qualifications.

Faculty will need to raise many questions and have them responded to in an open and honest manner. If the faculty members have had adequate input in the development of a *Qualifications Handbook*, much of their apprehension and fears will be removed. The system must be strong enough to eliminate, or put into a "probationary status," some faculty "competencies" or areas of previous teaching in which individuals really are not properly prepared to teach or to render a service to students. It must also be strong enough to withstand the pains of staff reduction and to come out on top in behalf

4

Board Policies in the Development of an Administrative Evaluation System

IN MANY COLLEGES AND SECONDARY SCHOOLS, administrators have found a relatively easy answer to the question of "Do you evaluate your faculty?" They have selected a student evaluation system to handle this problem in order to answer the question in the affirmative. In no other phase of personnel or other key management functions of the college does the administration and board of trustees relegate the decision making to their students!

Boards of trustees and boards of education do not relegate curriculum development, choice of textbooks, hiring of faculty, teacher assignments, ordering of classroom supplies, etc., to students. Why then do they allow their number-one quality check, faculty classroom evaluation, to be put into the hands of their students? Research shows that student evaluation is the number-one faculty evaluation method being used in both senior and junior and community colleges. It also shows little evidence of faculty having to be remediated in terms of their poor teaching practices and no evidence that faculty are fired due to their student evaluations.

48

A similar pattern exists with peer evaluation. Very little negative information is ever put into the written word by faculty evaluating their peers. Over 94 percent evaluate their colleagues as excellent to good. Research also points to a very low reliability between evaluations of peers when more than one peer is involved in evaluating the same instructor.

Shipka (1977) pointed out many of the intricate concerns that help to neutralize the impact of peer evaluation reviews:

> Understandably, advocates of peer review will say that the recommendations of peer committees reflect conscientious academic judgments, not the whims of the members. Given the modus operandi of peer committees, however, it is not easy to prove this claim. Such committees usually meet in executive session, keep perfunctory minutes if any, and state no rationale for their recommendations (p. 41).

Evertson and Holley (1981) stress that the very successful use of observation in classroom research "leaves no doubt" that classroom observation can provide a reasonable degree of reliability in the measurement of effective teaching. They go on to point out that "a picture of what effective teaching looks like in the classroom is starting to emerge, and the assessment of teachers by means of observation can now be regarded as a meaningful activity." They go on to point out that successful observation includes the interactive process with the teacher, students, and the classroom environmental variables (p. 107).

Secondary School Boards of Education, Community College Boards of Trustees, and Four-Year College Trustees are in unique positions to set the tone for administrative faculty evaluation systems with an emphasis on excellence. Through their policy setting powers, these governing boards can provide administrators with the framework and the strength to outline evaluation procedures that can measure the degree of excellence being provided by teachers in the classroom and in other professional job responsibilities. These same boards are often the final authority in the hiring of the college president, other administrators, and faculty, and in the granting of tenure and in the firing of any of these personnel. Governing boards derive their powers from several sources: the legislature, the constitution, state boards of education, or powers inferred therefrom (Piele, 1981). Discretionary powers are those powers which are not specifically spelled out from the above sources. Piele points out that courts have not usually interfered with a board's discretion unless "it's actions are clearly unreasonable, illegal, arbitrary, or capricious" (p. 8). Piele (1975) states that, as a matter of law in most states, discretionary powers are not delegable. It is a matter of common law in others. One example is that the board hires and the board fires and such power cannot be delegated. In the area of school boards' discretion to dismiss and/or discipline teachers, courts carefully observe required elements of due process and the proving of the charges. The courts have, however, supported boards and their administrators when they have brought forth strong cases. They check to make sure the board has stayed within its jurisdiction, and that there is no prejudicial abuse of discretion (Piele, 1981, p. 63)[1].

The right to establish policy is almost absolute for boards of education. Piele (1973) points out how courts must give great weight to boards' decisions affecting students, faculty, or academic offerings. He says the courts may believe that "any decision against a board may so undercut its respect and authority in other critical areas that all doubts should be resolved in favor of the governing body." He cites the majority of cases in the 1973 yearbook as support of this inference (p. 187).

Evertson and Holley (1981) support the need to strengthen classroom evaluation methods. They point out that classroom observations of five to ten minutes are the standard (p. 96). How can one critically capture any of the teacher's preparation level, interaction, questioning, adequate coverage of material, future assignments, and expectations of students in this type of observation? Some of the requirements they suggested as necessary for a school to have in place in an evaluation system that will be used in the termination of staff are as follows:

The publicity requirement obviously suggests that teachers should be informed that employment decisions will depend upon the results of their evaluations. But, more important, the school system's personnel policies should specify in appropriate detail the types of evaluation findings that are likely to lead to termination. The generality and regularity requirements suggest that all teaching personnel should be evaluated. (p. 313)

Caskin (1983), Cohen (1974), and Mark (1977) all suggest that evaluation systems usually have multiple purposes. Cohen suggests that an evaluation system cannot be both evaluatory and developmental. He stated that "one faculty evaluation system cannot both judge and assist (p. 12)." Mark points out that there is little research to support this claim or to show how the two goals of evaluation can be separated (p. 167).

Whether a college is using faculty assessment techniques for evaluation or for development purposes, Arreola (1983) points out that these techniques will always be viewed by faculty with a degree of apprehension, suspicion, fear, anxiety, resentfulness, and hostility (p. 85). Some of the faculty concerns that Arreola points to as common are:

1. Students aren't competent to evaluate me!

2. Teaching is too complex an activity to be evaluated validly!

3. You can't reduce something as complex as an evaluation of my performance to a number—some things just can't be measured!

He points out the inconsistency in this last faculty concern as it relates to faculty grading students: "Faculty consistency reduce the evaluation of complex student learning achievement to numbers; and based on those numbers, colleges award credit and degrees. As a profession we are not inexperienced in the process of summarizing evaluations of complex behaviors as numerical values (p. 85-89)."

Cooper, Andrews and Marzano have focused on the psychological needs of faculty in evaluation. Cooper

(1978, p. 382) found that the highly effective teachers in a junior college may be the ones who have the "greatest morale and job satisfaction." All three agree that those persons who are effective need feedback and administrative evaluation should let all faculty know how they stand within an institution.

For effective evaluation by administrators to take place, governing boards need to provide an attitude of support for the outcomes of the evaluation process. If the college president or the high school superintendent provides adequate evaluative documentation to warrant a "notice to remedy defects and deficiencies" or a recommendation for dismissal of a faculty member, a true test of a school system's evaluation system will be presented. The response of boards at these very delicate points of decision will provide the acid test for future evaluations. Positive support at these times will provide the motivation necessary for administrators to continue to carry out this type of job responsibility. Negative support shown by a decision of the board to not support a well documented recommendation will signal administrators to ask the question "Who needs it?" in reference to the very difficult job of documenting and attempting to change poor instructional patterns and performances of individual faculty members. Negative board responses will also send a clear signal to the faculty as a group that "a wide range of teaching performances will be tolerated in this college including those well below the average."

A governing board can also provide much momentum and support for a merit recognition system for those faculty members evaluated as providing outstanding instruction and other professional services to the college. Recognition for such merit consideration can be documented through the same evaluation process used to document poor instruction.

The following is recommended as a governing board's "overall" policy relative to evaluation and the expectation of quality in the classroom and in other job responsibilities:

Board Policy—Evaluation of Faculty Assistants to Instruction, and Counselors: Tenured, Non-tenured, and Part-time

It is the policy of the Board of Trustees that all faculty of the college shall be evaluated by their supervisors in order to assure that *quality* in instruction and other professional conduct is maintained.

Persons to be covered by the above mentioned evaluation procedures will be: (1) tenured faculty; (2) non-tenured faculty; (3) part-time faculty; (4) counselors; and (5) assistants to instruction.

MOVING TOWARD "QUALITY" LEVELS OF MINIMUM QUALIFICATIONS

One of the first steps a college or secondary school can take in insuring a high level of "quality" in the classroom is to develop appropriate board policies and procedures. The following are suggested board policy statements which should begin setting up the framework necessary for the hiring of well qualified professional staff, and for the continuation of the best qualified and competent instructors at times when reduction in force may be necessary due to shifting or declining student enrollments.

In regard to employment and the granting of tenure Rood (1977) points out: "Employment contracts and tenure are often, by statute, the prerogative solely of the board and are not subject to further delegation (p. 125)."

The first suggested board policy sets the "parameters" that are necessary to assure that a quality professional staff is hired. This policy is similar to those found in many community colleges where boards of trustees can set the standard:

Board Policy—Hiring of Professional Staff

The Board of Trustees will hire a professional staff, educated and prepared in accordance with generally accepted standards and practices for teaching in the discipline and subject fields to which they are assigned. These include collegiate study and/or professional experience. As a general rule, graduate work to the Master's Degree or beyond in the subjects or fields taught is expected except in such subjects and fields in which college programs are not normally available or in which the work experience and related training is the principal teaching medium.

The next board policy focuses in on "faculty and acadmic support personnel minimum qualifications and competencies:"

Board Policy—Establishing Competencies of Full-time Faculty and Instructional Support Personnel

The administration will establish and maintain a listing of minimum qualifications and competencies for each full-time faculty and academic support personnel.

This policy establishes the administration's role and responsibility in developing a "Handbook of Minimum Qualifications." The following board policy spells out the board's legal power in the releasing of non-tenured faculty members:

Board Policy –Decision Not to Rehire Non-tenured, Full-time and Instructional Support Personnel

A decision to not rehire (dismiss) a non-tenured faculty member for the ensuing school year or term will be made by the Board of Trustees reviewing the President's recommendation.

SUCCESSFUL IMPLEMENTATION OF BOARD POLICIES ON EVALUATION

Governing boards' policies as outlined above provide only the framework for a faculty evaluation system. The quality of the administrators and the procedures that are developed to carry out the board policies will determine now successful the policies will be. It is imperative that quality administrators, properly educated, trained, and experienced in good teaching techniques and methodologies be used in the evaluation system. Faculty have good cause to be concerned if an administrator without quality teaching experience becomes an evaluator. In any institution, a team approach to evaluation should prove to provide a higher degree of validity to the system than a single administrator carrying out such tasks.

Administrative personnel and faculty must all develop an understanding of the process that will be used and have a knowledge of the outcomes that may be forthcoming from an administrative evaluation system. It becomes important to an evaluator to understand various teaching styles and methodologies. The instructor's performance must be examined objectively and evaluated in light of the effectiveness of the particular instructor using his or her own choice of style and teaching methodologies.

When department chairpersons, division chairpersons, and/or deans of instruction evaluate the same faculty members in the same settings, using the same evaluation instrument, it is expected that two or three evaluators will find many similarities in their evaluations. It is this type of validity that is necessary for a successful administrative evaluation system.

Faculty who are evaluated positively should be complimented and given positive reinforcement. Those who are not properly prepared and are evaluated negatively should be made aware of any defects and/or deficiencies in their performance. This should be followed by a plan of action to remediate those identified defects. If the defects and deficiencies continue to exist and are picked up in subsequent administrative evaluations, movement toward a formal notice to remedy or toward firing the faculty member may be in order. It should be noted here that the vast majority of faculty evaluations should result in positive evaluation reports.

Brown (1977) points out that before the 1970s the courts had very little involvement in the resolution of disputes relative to the legal aspects of the academic tenure system. He goes on to describe the action since that time as an "explosion of litigation in the areas of tenure and employment contracts (p. 279)."

There will be check points for governing boards throughout the evalution process. Hiring, granting of tenure, dismissal of non-tenured staff, formal notice to remedy, merit recognition, and firing of tenured staff are all prerogatives and/or legal responsibilities of governing boards.

In a Colorado case, the board was considering not renewing a faculty member's contract and held a hearing to investigate the facts prior to making its final determination.[2] The teacher brought suit indicating the board "had prejudiced itself by the investigation." The court supported the board by saying:

> Under statutes providing for consideration of charges against school teacher by board of education, the board of education must not, prior to a hearing, so thoroughly investigate the matter as to render the subsequent statutory hearing superfluous, but the board may properly conduct a limited preliminary investigation to determine if there is any real substance to the charge against the teacher in order to avoid unnecessary embarrassment to the teacher and to avoid a waste of time; but the board must do nothing in the preliminary inquiry that would serve to remove the appearance of fairness from its eventual determination.[3]

BEYOND THE CALL ... STATUTORY INTERFERENCE

Legislators in several states have introduced and enacted statutes that provide faculty protections beyond those that are required by the constitution. The need to provide a statement of reason in the non-renewal of a non-tenured faculty member's contract is one. Requiring a pretermination hearing before an independent hearing officer is another.

In Kentucky, a statute requires, on request, that a faculty member must be given a written statement of the grounds for the decision (Piele, 1981, p. 89). Similar statutes have been established in Alaska and Vermont. In Illinois, the 1984 legislative session introduced "peer evaluation" as a clause to be included in faculty contracts under the newly enacted (January 1, 1984) collective bargaining legislation. Whether such legislation passes or not is still to be determined. It is one further example of an attempt to erode board's rights and responsibilities to determine the best means to evaluate faculty for retention, promotion or dismissal.

Arreola (1983) also placed the role of faculty evaluation near the center of importance for effective instructional administration when he stated:

> Only when the administration realizes that well-constructed faculty evaluation and development programs do not diminish their ability to direct the course and quality of their institutions, but rather enhance and strengthen it, will a truly successful faculty evaluation and development program have been established. (p. 92)

He also alludes to the need for faculty evaluation to be systematic, fair, and carried out in a predictable manner if it is to succeed. Boards of trustees should expect nothing less from its administration in carrying out such an important program for the college. The pay-offs in quality instruction, faculty morale, and high student learning are stakes that are too high to gamble with in a less than superb manner. While administrators want support by the board of trustees or board of education for their recommendations on faculty and other staff, it is just as important for a governing board to expect and receive high quality input from its administrative leaders in order to make some sound personnel decisions.

Lewis (1980) suggests that college presidents should assist board members through "instruction" in their role as policy makers:

> If you do decide to help us, be expansive and generous, and give us a little more instruction. Tell us that our primary

duty is to determine and, if necessary, redetermine the
mission and purpose of our college, and that only in that
context do we really involve ourselves with "policy"—
policy related to the delivery of excellent education services
at the classroom (or equivalent) level is, above all else, our
raison d'eire. (p. 20)

SUMMARY

It is important for governing boards to be committed
to excellence in instruction and related instructional
services if an administrative evaluation system is to exist
and succeed. This chapter presented some possible board
policies which can set up a framework for administrative
evaluation procedures to be developed.

Governing boards also need to have an attitude of
support for administrative recommendations in the carrying out of the board policies and procedures. Decisions
in hiring of staff, board support of outstanding performances, reprimands, notices to remedy defects and deficiencies, recommendations for tenure, and recommendations not to grant tenure all come before governing trustees.
A solid administrative evaluation system may ask for
support in terms of merit recognition or, on the other
extreme, ask for support of a recommendation to dismiss
a tenured faculty member.

The board policies and administrative follow-up of
these policies, to be successful, will depend in no small
way upon the attitude and commitment to excellence
a board of trustees or board of education wants to make.

CHAPTER 4 ENDNOTES

[1] See generally Hughes v. Board of Educ., 599 S.W.3d 254
(mo. Ct. App. 1980), where a school board's failure to make findings
of fact in support of a dismissal decision was error justifying reinstatement, and Board of Trustees of Garfield Cty. High School v.
Eaton, 605 P.2d 1083 (Mont. 1979), where a school board's dismissal of a principal failed to conform to procedural requirements of
state law.

[2] Weissman v. Board of Educ. of Jefferson Cty. School District.,
547 P.2d 1267 (Colo. 1978); Griggs v. Board of Trustees of Merced

Union High School Dist., 389 P.2d 722 (Cal. 1964); Phillips v.
Board of Educ. of Smyrea School Dist., 330 A.2d 151 (Super. Ct.
Del. 1974); Million v. Board of Educ. of Wichita, 310 P.2d 917
(Kan. 1957); Petitions of Davenport, 283 A.2d 452 (Vt. 1971);
Simard v. Board of Educ. of Town of Croton, 473 F.2d 988 (2d.
Cir. 1973); Swab v. Cedar Rapids Commun. School Dist., 494
F.2d 353 (8th Cir. 1974); cf. King v. Caesar Rodney School Dist.,
380 F. Supp. 1112 (D.C. Del. 1974); Goldberg v. Kelly, 397 U.S.
254; Tyson v. New York Housing Authority, 369 F. Supp. 513
(D.C. N.Y. 1974); Gilbertson v. McAlister, 383 F. Supp. 1107
(D.C. Conn. 1974); In re Flannery's Appeal, 178 A.2d 751 (Pa.
1962); Colorado Springs v. District Ct., 519 P.2d 325 (Colo. 1974);
and Bauch v. Anderson, 49/P.2d 598 (Color. 1972).

[3]ld.

5

"Teaching is too important to too many to be conducted without a critical inquiry into its worth."

Millman, 1981

Evaluating Non-Tenured Faculty

HIRING OF NEW PERSONNEL into a college or secondary education type of institutional setting can be a most invigorating and rewarding experience. A new faculty member can provide some new, refreshing reflections to the college from outside experiences, up-to-date educational preparation, and/or freshness in approach to the institution.

Most new persons hired by an institution should be brought in already possessing the *minimum qualifications* that have been established for the position by the college in its board of trustee policies.

Documenting the minimum qualifications through a candidate's personnel file, placement papers, reference letters, and follow-up telephone calls to references and previous employers is only the first step. It is *after* the person begins work in an individual school that evaluation toward competence in that particular institution can begin.

Bevan (1980) suggests strongly that "the most important responsibility, that of monitoring the development of a colleague and keeping that colleague informed, seems to be the one regularly neglected." He points out that workshops to train department chairpersons "are sorely needed (p. 14)."

NON-TENURED EVALUATION PROCESS

This section will outline a model that may be used in the evaluation of non-tenured faculty, assistants to instruction, and counselors. Such evaluation should evolve around each institution's own "strawperson" or image of what makes up excellence in instruction or other professional positions. Chapter 4 outlined some possible board of trustee policies related to the hiring and evaluation of faculty and academic support members. This board policy was suggested for evaluation:

Board Policy – Evaluation of Faculty, Assistants to Instruction, and Counselors: Tenured, Non-tenured, and Part-time

It is the policy of the Board of Trustees that all faculty of the college shall be evaluated by their supervisors in order to assure that quality in instruction, in other professional duties, and in professional conduct is maintained.

The following procedure for non-tenured faculty evaluation is proposed as a model. It can be used by administrators who will have responsibilities in evaluating in classrooms and overall job responsibilities and conduct of non-tenured employees.

NON-TENURED EVALUATION

Procedures for the Evaluation of All Full-Time Non-Tenured Faculty, Assistants to Instruction, and Counselors

It is the responsibility of the administration to implement the following procedures which will provide for the evaluation of *all full-time non-tenured* faculty, assistants to instruction, and counselors:

1. The Division Chairpersons, Dean of Instruction, Principal (or his representative) will evaluate classes or

labs of each non-tenured instructor and/or assistant to instruction in the college.

2. The Dean of Student Development will evaluate counseling sessions, career workshops, classes or seminars of non-tenured counselors.

3. The Division Chairpersons, Dean of Instruction, Principal (or his representative), or Dean of Student Development (for counselors) will also evaluate all other aspects of the jobs to be performed by faculty, assistants to instruction, and counselors. The criteria that will be used in the evaluation process in addition to classroom or other formal activity (depending upon an instructor's teaching assignment and/or a counselor's assignments) will include:
   a. Advisory committee work in programs.
   b. Maintaining curriculum, course updates, and revisions.
   c. College committee work.
   d. Maintaining records as required by law, college policy, and administrative regulations.
   e. Maintaining scheduled office hours.
   f. Attending and participating in faculty and division meetings.

4. A formal evaluation conference with the Division Chairperson, Dean of Instruction, or Principal (or Dean of Student Development for counselors) and the faculty member will be held within a reasonable time period following a classroom visitation and/or evaluation filed on the other job performance criteria that are outlined above. The conference should be held within one to five working days following such evaluation.

5. A faculty member, assistant to instruction, or counselor will be appraised of any defects and/or deficiencies in his or her performance as discovered in the formal evaluation process. The person evaluated will be advised to take appropriate action to remediate the defects/ deficiencies cited.

6. Division Chairpersons will evaluate non-tenured staff a minimum of twice a semester during the first year of employment.

7. Division Chairpersons will evaluate non-tenured staff a minimum of once a semester during the second and third years of employment or until tenure is conferred.

8. The Dean of Instruction, Principal (or his representative), will evaluate non-tenured staff no less than once a year as a minimum.

9. All evaluation visits will be made unannounced to the staff member involved.

10. Any faculty member, assistant to instruction, or counselor who has been employed in the college or secondary school for a period of three successful consecutive school years shall be eligible for tenure. Recommendations for tenure will be made by the Division Chairperson in consultation with the Dean of Instruction or Principal to the college President or school Superintendent. The Dean of Student Development will recommend tenure ot the college President or Principal for counselors.

11. The President or Superintendent will review recommendations for tenure and make his or her recommendations to the Board of Trustees or Board of Education.

12. This evaluation procedure recognizes that only the board has the authority by law to confer tenure.

13. The board may, however, at its option, extend such period (non-tenure) for one additional school year by giving the faculty member notice not later than 60 days before the end of the school year, or term during the school year, or term immediately preceding the school year, or term in which tenure would otherwise be conferred.

14. If the implementation of the above formal evaluation system results in a decision to dismiss a non-tenured staff member (as named in this section) for the ensuing school year or term, the board shall give notice therof to the faculty member not later than 60 days before the end of the school year or term. The specific reasons for the dismissal shall be confidential but shall be issued to the teacher upon request.

15. If a decision to dismiss a non-tenured staff member is made, all requirements as outlined in the College or Secondary School Tenure Act, "Dismissal of Non-Tenured Faculty Member" will be followed.

An administrative evaluation form to accompany this "non-tenured" evaluation process is presented as Appendix A.

DEALING WITH LESS THAN MINIMUM QUALIFICATIONS

It was mentioned above that some persons who may be considered for hire may not possess all of the minimum *ideal* qualifications that the college or secondary school would like to have in the persons they hire. This may be due to a shortage of persons in a field at various times, competition from business and industry, and/or due to newly created positions.

A potential candidate for a position may be hired if the institution is willing to initially *waive* one or more of the minimum qualifications. It should be decided prior to employment if the qualification(s) can be made up or accomplished within a reasonable period of time. In those institutions with a probationary period that leads to a tenure position possibility, a candidate should be able to accomplish the waived qualifications within the two- or three-year probationary period. The requirement that is expected to be met should be outlined in the person's personal contract of employment:

*CONTRACT NOTE: Continued employment and movement toward tenure is contingent upon the attainment of a Master's Degree in Nursing.

The above type of requirement may be a minimum requirement of the school, the specific program, and/or accrediting agencies reviewing the program's status. Another example of a person who may not have the minimum qualifications in a specific field follows:

*CONTRACT NOTE: Continued employment and movement toward tenure is contingent upon obtaining an additional 15 semester hours of college credit in computer science and data processing courses.

Once it has been established that some minimum qualifications must be achieved before a faculty member is allowed to move into a tenured position, college administrators need to monitor progress toward the achievement of those qualifications:

Example 1:

"Your teaching techniques utilizing student participation as the nucleus of learning in your classroom appears to be very effective. Keep up the good work and *continue to work* toward your Master's Degree in nursing."

Example 2:

"We also discussed your need to continue your education in the C.S.L/D.P. area. Your knowledge in Fortran and BASIC is good but you need to become more versatile and bring your background in line with our minimum qualification requirements."

Some faculty will accomplish meeting the qualifications that have been outlined in a minimal amount of time. Requirements such as moving from a Bachelor's Degree to a Master's Degree will take some diligent planning and dedicated effort. Other faculty may, for whatever personal reasons, neglect to accomplish the requirements. The following is an example of an evaluation dealing with such a case by a dean of instruction:

"It is discouraging to note your lack of professional improvement in courses that would bring your background in line with the minimum qualifications required by the college for your position. You were advised of this requirement at the time you were hired and in three subsequent evaluations."

The above examples should serve to show the evaluator and board of trustees or board of education how some qualifications can be initially waived for a person entering a position and subsequently be monitored. It is also another means of evaluating the *total person* prior to a tenure decision.

MOVING TOWARD TENURE: POSITIVE EVALUATION

The *rewards* of high-quality-level qualifications, close employment screening for new positions, and an effective evaluation system will be forthcoming throughout the non-tenure years. Written and oral evaluation reviews should provide much needed reinforcement and sense of accomplishment for the competent faculty members and assistants to instruction. Such evaluations will clarify strengths, provide suggestions for improvements and document *overall* job performances. Some examples òf positive movement toward tenured status via evaluation are provided below:

Example 1:

"Over the past two and one-half years, this instructor has demonstrated the qualities of a superior instructor. She consistently utilizes student participation, compliments students for their responses and usually finds something good in a response even if it is not exactly correct."

Example 2:

"This instructor has made an excellent adaptation of her previous experience and training for our students' needs. She, in turn, is sympathetic to their problems, encourages them in constructively critical ways, and fields their questions with thorough, but not tedious, explanations. She is considerably more confident and thus more relaxed in the classroom than last year."

Both of the above examples show elements of positive growth documented through evaluation by administrators.

MOVEMENT TOWARD TENURE

The granting of tenure by a board traditionally provides a faculty member the most substantial property right in employment that can be conveyed by a board policy or by a state statute law. Piele (1981) says "tenure laws are based largely on state statute, are specific to each state jurisdiction, thus the variation of each state's judicial interpretation may often be predicated on the nuances of each state's statute law" (pp. 83-84).

In many colleges and secondary schools, the movement toward a tenured position calls for a probationary period of two or three years. The Community College Tenure Act in Illinois went into effect in January of 1980. It calls for a tenure decision to be made no less than 60 days before the end of the sixth semester of employment. It does, however, provide for a possible extension into a fourth year at the discretion of the board of trustees and with notice being given no less than 60 days prior to the end of the third year of non-tenure status.

The college administrators involved in each individual case are expected to weigh all of the evaluation evidence in making its decision on whether to recommend tenure or possible dismissal. A recommendation should go to the president for review before being taken before the board of trustees.

The following are recommendation statements that may summarize a three-year probationary period for an instructor:

"Based upon consistently excellent classroom teaching evaluations, renovation of a faltering program, innovative reorganization of traditional courses, completion of a master's degree program, and continuing participation in professional and community activities, this report will recommend highly that the instructor be granted tenure by the Board of Trustees.

"Similarly, the instructor has been helpful to her chairperson in revising every syllabus in her curriculum. Her suggestions have given new substance to those courses."

The recommendation for tenure should be a composite recommendation of those persons who have been involved in the administrative evaluation process.

MOVEMENT TOWARD TERMINATION: NEGATIVE EVALUATION

Some faculty and academic support personnel will present the minimum qualifications, positive experience references and come through the screening process and be hired... only to prove later that they have personality defects or are unable or unwilling to respond to suggested changes necessary to move toward a tenured position. An objective administrative evaluation system will be able to properly document such behavior. The following examples are used to show how negative evaluation raises *doubts* about a person's long-term adjustment possibilities to a college or secondary school:

Example 1:

"This instructor needs to put more time and effort into the preparation, organization and presentation of the lecture material. The instructor needs to motivate himself to be more enthusiastic and conscientious in teaching his subject."

Example 2:

(This example is for an assistant to instruction position, laboratory assistant.)
"1. Supplies have not been requested on time, thereby causing adjustments in laboratory sequences;
"2. Although you have been informed that student lab assistants under your supervision should be working at all times, I frequently find them just sitting or talking to students;
"3. You have been late to some 10:00 a.m. labs and left some early without permission.
"You are urged to come in for a meeting and express some remedial procedures for these deficiencies."

Example 3:

"As an instructional administrator, I would define good instructor-student relationships in a classroom to center around mutual respect which can be observed in (1) attendance, (2) promptness, (3) instructor preparation, (4) notetaking, and (5) questions to and from students relative to the class topic. NONE OF THESE WERE OBSERVED."

In each of the three examples above, the instructors and assistant to instruction have been evaluated to show some patterns of behavior that make them suspect to on-going quality instruction and academic support services.

MOVEMENT TOWARD TERMINATION

There will be some questionable teaching and/or other job behavior that will raise doubts in the movement toward tenure. Such behavior should be observed, documented, and thoroughly discussed with the faculty or academic support person involved. Attempts should be made to remediate the questionable behavior. It is important that such behavior be validated through subsequent classroom or other observation techniques being used. When it persists over a period of time, the administrative evaluators should be aware that they will have to decide on the severity of the behavior as it relates to a tenure decision.

The following are example of behavior that makes a tenure recommendation difficult:

Example 1:

"This instructor has continually refused to comply with his supervisor's request to take additional coursework in his field. He has not demonstrated a willingness to be directed in this area."

Example 2:

"I was very disappointed with your lecture today. Many of my suggestions have been made several times after previous classroom evaluations.

"1. Be prepared."

"2. The class lecture moved very slowly. You were not properly prepared to lecture in an organized manner, students didn't appear to have read the material before class, and you relied almost entirely on reading from the text."

The above examples show patterns of behavior that have not been remediated over a period of time. Each instructor has received both oral and written evaluations on these concerns. Whether such behavior is considered insubordination or incompetent is irrelevant in such cases. It is important to the overall quality of institutions that such behavior is not allowed to continue. The probationary non-tenure period is the time to sort out these behaviors and severe ties with such faculty and academic support personnel.

THE DISMISSAL PROCESS

Strike and Bull (1981, p. 321) have summarized the following as *generalizations* relative to the *legal status* of non-tenured teachers:

1. Probationary teachers have no property interest in their continued employment. They will not, therefore, receive the protection of federal courts under the due process clause of the 14th amendment. Federal courts will interject themselves into the nonrenewal of a non-tenured teacher only when the grounds of dismissal are not constitutionally permissible.

2. Some states have extended minimal components of due process to probationary teachers. Most common are the right to a statement of the grounds for nonrenewal and the right to respond.

3. Additional rights may be secured by contract. Relevant provisions include appeals procedures, grievance procedures, provisions about the teacher's file, and rights to notice and appeal.

4. There is little in state law or contractual provisions that specifies grounds for nonrenewal.

It is of utmost importance that the colleges and secondary schools follow very closely the time frames provided for in a tenure act, faculty contract, or other documents governing the dismissal of a non-tenured person. It is possible for a non-tenured person to automatically obtain tenure in some states if the notification date of "intention not to rehire" is not met. Notification of *intent not to rehire* can be made by the college president to the person involved prior to official board of trustees action. The next step is board action on the recommendation. The person in question may wish to submit a letter of resignation prior to the president's or superintendent's recommendation to terminate the employee. A resignation allows for a faculty or academic support member to save some face with his or her colleagues and avoid a public firing. It may provide a better chance to move to another job.

It is possible, by board of trustee action, to extend a faculty or academic support person an additional probationary year. Such a decision might be made for a person who has shown outstanding promise in the institution but has been unable to complete a qualification requirement.

WHEN IN DOUBT . . .

The non-tenure probationary period for faculty and academic support personnel gives the college or secondary school an excellent opportunity to *guarantee* high quality personnel for the institution. A thorough screening process at the time of hiring followed by one, two, and/or three years of close evaluation should give an institution a chance to make solid decisions on the retention of highly competent personnel. It also allows administrators and boards a chance to start over when a person has created doubt about the quality of her or her performance. *When in doubt, it is a good practice to release a person before placing the person into a tenure status.*

Governing boards in most states have a wide number of discretionary reasons to dismiss such teachers. On the other hand, state statute limits the rights probationary teachers may claim as compared to teachers who are in continued employment (Piele, 1981). Two cases in Ohio were decided in favor of boards which faculty members charged had violated the "Sunshine Law." The court ruled against the teachers' claim stating, "A non-tenured teacher has no expectancy of continued employment past the term of his limited contract" (p. 84). The court also ruled in favor of the board in relation to the "Sunshine Law" charge. The court said, "Boards of education have the power to go into closed session when discussing an employee's status." It went on to say, "The statute does not grant non-tenured teachers a right to demand that a school board conduct all its deliberations on contract renewals in open session.[1]

One decision of the Fifth Circuit Court of Appeals eventually reached the United States Supreme Court. The Supreme Court ruled that "where there is neither tenure nor an expectancy of re-employment, the teacher must bear the burden of both initiating the proceedings and of proving that a wrong has been done by the action of the college in not rehiring him, since without the existence of tenure or expectancy of re-employment, the college may base its decision relative to such re-employment upon any reason or no reason at all."[2]

Further, the court declared that "if a teacher determines to assert that a nonrenewal of his contract is a punishment for his exercise of constitutional rights or otherwise constitutes some actionable wrong, he may request and be afforded a proper hearing before an appropriate tribunal consistent with appropriate procedural due process guarantees as outlined in Ferguson."[3]

In a Michigan case, the question of whether or not reasons, or cause, needed to be given in a denial of tenure case was raised (Piele, 1980, p. 84):

> The primary issue in the Michigan case was whether or not reasons must be given for denial of tenure. The state supreme court was evenly divided in a previous hearing of the case.[4] In this instance, one of the justices changed his vote, and the majority now held that reasons need not be stated.[5] Citing Roth,[6] the court concluded that there was no entitlement under the state tenure act (p. 84).

A New Jersey case challenged one board's dismissal decision by pointing to improper reasons for the instructor's dismissal (Knowles and Wedlock, 1973):

> A New Jersey court refused to look into a non-tenured instructor's claim that a college's decision not to renew his contract was based on his activities directed toward organizing the college's faculty and his position as the salary negotiator for those faculty members who had organized.[7] The instructor claimed that his nonretention was based upon his exercise of lawful union activities and thus violated his First Amendment rights. The court, in holding against the instructor, felt that to hold otherwise would be tantamount to abolishing the tenure system. It further stated that:

> . . . inherent in our legislatively enacted tenure policy is the existence of a probationary period during which the board will have a chance to evaluate a teacher with no commitments to re-employ him.[8]

The court concluded that:

> . . . we hold that it is the prerogative of the board of trustees to discontinue the employment of a non-tenured teacher at the end of his teaching contract with or without reason.[9]

The following case also put the burden of proof upon the professor (Knowles and Wedlock, 1973):

> The Court of Appeals for the First Circuit, while affirming a district court's order to a college to provide a statement of reasons for nonrenewal of a non-tenured professor's contract, applied the arbitrary-and-capricious standard.[10] The professor was saddled with proving that the college's reasons for not retaining him were trivial and unrelated to the educational process or to working relations within the college, or in the alternative, totally unsupported by the facts. He failed. The court upheld nonrenewal of his contract based upon the reasons that he was "difficult to get along with" as well as "a threat to the harmony" of the department.[11] (p. 205).

A decision by the board in a New Mexico case was reversed when the board did not follow its own board-approved procedure:

> In a case arising in New Mexico, it was held that where a faculty handbook, which had been approved by the Regents, was treated as the controlling relationship between a professor and the university and was part of his contract, the

failure of the University to follow the procedures set forth in the handbook concerning his treatment as a first year faculty member who was not reappointed, constituted a breach of contract by the University.[12] It was held that the professor had an "expectation of re-employment." (Peterson and Garver, 1972, p. 220).

A charge, made by a Mississippi faculty member, that an evaluation system was not *objective* was not supported by the court (Piele, 1975):

> A non-tenured teacher was nonrenewed in Mississippi on charges of poor classroom performance and lack of pupil control. The teacher charged that the evaluation system was not objective and thus violated his Fourteenth Amendment rights. The court held that Singleton rules did not apply, that the system had been operating as a unitary school system for seven semesters, and that the teacher's nonrenewal was not related to faculty reorganization. The teacher also had a full year's warning regarding the inadequacy of his performance.
> The court further held that the evaluation form did not violate Fourteenth Amendment rights: . . . That the form may contain a certain degree of 'subjectivity,' and is not wholly or purely 'objective,' in a reasonable effort to measure a teacher's classroom performance, does not offend the Equal Protection Clause, absent invidious discrimination. Neither does the mechanism of the evaluation procedure, in which the teacher, the principal, and two fellow teachers (of both races) participated, run afoul of the Due Process Clause. This court is content to leave the concerns for improving the quality of instructors in the public schools to the lawfully constituted officials charged with that important public duty."[13]
> The Board's decision was affirmed[14] (p. 167).

The above case was a victory for the use of an evaluation form by administrators. It also provided additional support for the idea that schools should be in charge of "improving the quality of instructors."

In a case involving *Cook County College Teachers Union Local 1600 v. Byrd,* 456 F. 2d 822 (1972), the court ruled that the college must have:

> ". . . a very wide spectrum of reasons from subtle and difficult to articulate and to demonstrate, for deciding not to retain a newcomer or one who had not yet won sufficient respect from his colleagues . . ." (456 F. 2d 882 at 889).

The court concluded, stating:

> ". . . it is not our function to evaluate a professor's competence nor to determine whether he any longer fits the needs or a school that is expanding its programs and attempting to upgrade the quality of its faculty. We may not so far involve this court in the discretionary decisions made by state-controlled colleges" (456 F. 2d 882 at 889).

Non-tenured teachers and academic support persons do not have the same constitutionally-protected property interest as tenured personnel are afforded. Strike and Bull (1981, p. 314) point to two comparison cases where this distinction was first clearly activated:

> In *Board of Regents v. Roth* (1972), a non-tenured university teacher whose contract was not renewed at year's end was held to have no such interest and, therefore, not to deserve formal termination proceedings.[13]

In the second comparison case the following was decided:

> In *Perry v. Sinderman* (1972), the second companion case, a teacher with 10 years experience within the state college system of Texas was held to have a constitutionally protected property interest in his job even though there was no explicit provision for tenure in Texas statutory law. Here the Court found that the contract renewal practice in effect in the college system implicitly conferred upon long-term employees a legitimate expectation of future employment, which constituted a property interest sufficient to require formal procedures.[14]

In *Board of Trustees of Community College District Number 513 v. Dale Krizek and the American Federation of Teachers, Local 1810* (1983), the Third District Appellate Court of Illinois pointed out the *power* that is vested with a governing board.[15] They started by citing from previous cases:

> First, in *Board of Education of the City of Chicago v. Chicago Teachers Union, Local 1* (1981), 88 Ill. 2d 63, 430 N.E. 2d 1111; *Board of Trustees v. Cook County College Teachers Union, Local 1600* (1976), 63 Ill. 2d 470, 343 N.E. 2d 473; and *Illinois Education Association v. Board of*

Education (1975), 62 Ill. 2d 127, 340 N.E. 2d 7, the supreme court has made unmistakably clear that when a governing board is vested with the power to grant tenure, or to not renew, then the governing board cannot delegate, modify or condition its final authority to make such decisions. Although the statute here in question differs slightly from the one at issue in the prior cases, there is no variation from the essential factor relied on in those cases, i.e., *the governing board's ultimate authority on tenure questions. There can be no dilution of the board's authority whether the evaluation of teachers is mandated by contract or by statute* [emphasis added]. It follows then that the power to grant tenure cannot be conditioned upon the decision of an administrator to make a recommendation or hold a consultation, not can the power be limited by the preponderance of opinion of evaluators, even though their evaluations may be conducted at the behest of the board. So long as a procedure for evaluation has been implemented, and the results of those evaluations are available to the board, we believe that compliance with the statute has been achieved, and any subsequent decisions to terminate ordered by the board are statutorily sound.

We are mindful that the tenure laws represent an elaborate balance between the need to maintain the quality of schools and the opposing interest in job security. *(Board of Education of the City of Chicago v. Chicago Teachers Union, Local 1* (J. Simon, dissenting).) In striking that balance, the legislature has crafted a system where there appears to be unlimited power in boards to dismiss probationary teachers at the board's discretion while the power to dismiss tenured teachers is considerably restricted. *(Lockport Area Special Education Cooperative v. Lockport Area Special Education Cooperative Association* (1975), 33 Ill. App. 3d 789, 338 N.E. 2d 463.) We perceive Krizek's position as an attempt to erode the area of the board's discretion by injecting elements of cause into the board's decision to terminate. Inasmuch as this is repugnant to the policy embodied in the statute, we decline to adopt the statutory construction proffered by Krizek.

Finally, in her brief Krizek raises a constitutional issue concerning infringement of her right to due process. Although the Board seeks to have those portions of the brief stricken as representing theories not pursued in the court below, we hereby deny the motion to strike, but dimiss the substantive issue raised by Krizek as without merit, relying on the authority of *Board of Trustees v. Cook County College Teachers Union, Local 1600,* which presented the same question for review in a factually indistinguishable setting.

We conclude, then, that the decision of the circuit court of LaSalle County was correct, and its judgment should be affirmed for the reasons we have set forth.

The process of dismissal of ineffective non-tenured personnel is relatively simple when compared to dismissal of tenured personnel. It should, however, evolve from a quality evaluation system. Arreola (1983) says, "Only when the administration realizes that well constructed faculty evaluation and development programs do not diminish their ability to direct the course and quality of their institutions, but rather enhance and strengthen it, will a truly successful faculty evaluation and development program have been established (p. 92)." Such should be the case in determining who should warrant tenure in a college or secondary school. An effective administrative evaluation system should provide the students and the board guarantees of long-term quality staff.

SUMMARY

Hiring a new faculty or academic support person into a college or secondary school can be an invigorating experience. It is also an excellent opportunity for the institution, through its high qualification standards, rigorous screening process, and a strong administrative evaluation/ improvement oriented process, to improve the institution. The attitude of the administrators and faculty involved in the screening process will help set the tone for the person's feelings toward the institution before his or her first day of work.

Evaluation for persons who are to be considered for continued employment, tenure, salary advancements, promotion opportunities and merit recognition should begin very early. Such evaluation will assist the person to know if his or her level of preparation, organization, student expectations, etc., are at the level the *individual* college or secondary school expects of its faculty or academic support personnel. It should lead to both oral and written evaluation reports for improvement, encouragement, and recognition of good efforts.

Reaction to evaluation will help provide the true test of how a person wants to fit into the institution. Positive reaction to suggestions and criticism followed by some action to remediate any defects or concerns is a good indication that the individual is concerned, flexible, and capable of improving his or her performance. Negative and defensive reactions, followed by a "business-as-before" attitude also warns an administrator about some important personality traits with which one should be concerned. The evaluation should be conducted around the "strawperson of excellence" developed in chapter 1 as a guide. The "strawperson" and the evaluation procedures need to be understood by those persons who will be evaluated.

Evaluation that leads to any doubt relative to a person's ability to fit in and work at the productivity level expected by the administration and board should lead to a relatively early parting of the faculty or academic support member. How much ease is involved in such a departure depends to a great degree on the person involved. A simple letter of resignation is the cleanest for both parties. A recommendation to fire may be necessary and a challenge in the courts may occasionally be expected. The "property right" issue that courts use in a tenured staff member's dismissal is not available for non-tenured staff members. The reasons for dismissal may need to be given but, boards have much greater powers and flexibility, in terms of the range of reasons that can be given, when dismissing a non-tenured faculty member.

In this chapter a look has been taken at both the positive and negative aspects of hiring and evaluating non-tenured staff members. The overwhelming amount of time in the process will involve guiding and praising satisfactory to exceptional job performances. Good administration will mean providing the support that is necessary to assist the good people to carry out their teaching and other job responsibilities with a minimum amount of disruption. Good administration also means *biting the bullet* on less than average to poor performing personnel. It means straight talk and written documentation on poor performances. It also means dismissing staff in order to improve the institution for the students who expect excellence to exist for them in all aspects of the college or secondary school they attend.

CHAPTER 5 ENDNOTES

[1]Matheny v. Frontier Local Bd. of Educ., 405 N.E. 2d 1041 (Ohio 1980). See also Unified School Dist. No. 461 v. Dice, 612 P.2d 1203 (Kan. 1980), where a school board's decision not to renew contract of a teacher employed since 1974 for the 1978-79 year was sustained.

[2]Sindermann v. Perry, 430 F. 2d 939 (Texas 1970).

[3]Ferguson v. Thomas 430 F. 2d 852 (Texas 1970).

[4]See Lipka v. Brown City Comm. Schools, 252 N.W.2d 770 (Mich. 1977), YEARBOOK 1978 at 116. See also YEARBOOK 1976 at 190-91.

[5]Lipka v. Brown City Commun. Schools, 271 N.W.2d 771 (Mich. 1978).

[6]Roth, supra note 2.

[7]Katz v. Board of Trustees of Gloucester County College, 118 N.J. Super. 398, 288 A.2d 43 (1972).

[8]Id. at 49.

[9]Id.

[10]McEnteggart v. Cataldo, 451 F.2d 1109 (1st Circ. 1971).

[11]Id. at 1111.

[12]Hillis v. Meister, 483 P. 2d 1314 (N. Mex. 1971).

[13]See Pickens, supra note 7 at 1043.

[14]See Pickens, supra note 7.

[15]Board of Regents v. Roth, 408 V.S. 564 (1972).

[16]Perry v. Sinderman, 408 V.S. 593 (1972).

[17]Krizek v. Board of Trsutees of Community College District No. 513, 445-447 N.E.2d 770 (Ill. 1983).

6

*In a Gallup Poll reflecting on
what the public thinks about the
educational system in America, some
71 percent would approve of
"changing the tenure or seniority
system to make it easier to fire poor teachers."*

Newsweek, 1983

Evaluating the "Untouchables"... Tenured Faculty

THE AURA OF THE GRANTING OF 'TENURE' to faculty members in community colleges and secondary schools has perpetuated a mystique similar to that with which the four-year college and university system has lived. The falsely perpetuated *job security* and 'untouchable' status granted to tenured faculty members is due in a large part to the naiveness and weaknesses of governing boards and administrators in understanding their policy-making and administrative-evaluation roles.

The very structure of educational institutions should help point out the need for a continuing evaluation system that covers tenured as well as non-tenured teaching faculty. For community college and secondary school faculty, teaching is the number one and often only priority. The granting of tenure is accomplished through administrative recommendations versus faculty committee recommendations at most four-year colleges and universities.

In criticizing evaluation systems, Bevan finds them usually at fault for not continuing evaluation of faculty once tenure is achieved. He says that it appears to be assumed that the level of accepted competence attained during the

probationary period will be "maintained and enhanced."
Brown (1977, p. 280) points out the "sometimes
apparent dichotomy" that exists between the theoretical
principle of tenure and its practical application:

> If there is any truth to the conception of tenure as
> unbreakable, it is because of institutional practices rather
> than because of precise protective doctrines developed by
> the courts. Nothing in the rationales, norms, or rules of
> tenure legally shields any faculty member from accountability
> for performance as teacher, scholar, and colleague.

Brown contends that the basic goal of tenure is "To
insure that faculty members will not be dismissed without
adequate cause and without due process."

During the early 1970s the AAUP reacted to outside
societal pressures regarding the tenure system by stressing
that "tenure is not impregnable, and that tenured faculty
members may be dismissed for cause." Nisbet (1973, p. 46),
in his strong critical analysis of the American university and
college tenure system, states:

> We should make clear at the outset what tenure is in
> actual operation in the American university and college. It
> is a guarantee by the institution to individual, irrespective
> of his age, of appointment until the time of retirement comes.
> Mental deterioration, sloth, abandonment of professional
> standards, gross immorality in or outside the university,
> flagrant breach of academic position, none of these on the
> evidence is likely to affect the permanence of appointment
> once tenure has been granted.

Nisbet responded to the AAUP statements by showing
that while they say tenure is not impregnable, "the record
refutes it." He points out that anyone can think of how many
persons they know who have taught and/or are teaching in
these universities and colleges who show signs of incompetence, deterioration, gross neglect of duty, etc., and ask
"how many tenured faculty members in this country have
ever in fact been dismissed for cause." He points out that
the number is minuscule and that records in many institutions would show that "no tenured individual has ever been
dismissed" (p. 47).

In his closing comments to AAUP's contentions, Nisbet

states that "to argue that tenure is not a refuge for the lazy, incompetent and delinquent, that 'with cause shown' such individuals may be dismissed, hardly carries conviction when, as the record makes plain, tenure *is* such a refuge" (p. 47).

Nielsen and Polishook (1983, p. 6) point out that "even the most loyal advocates in the struggle to maintain tenure are apt to forget that it is not an unconditional right." They go on to say that "what we generally overlook is that our conception of tenure as a right runs counter to the public view of tenure as a privilege."

The significance of tenure and the courts were discussed by Rood (1977, p. 132). He says that "the significance of tenure is widely misunderstood." He says that "for many, there is an erroneous inference that tenure carries a lifetime re-employment guarantee ... however, the courts have not interpreted tenure in this manner." He goes on to point out that the courts "recognize tenure only as the termination of a probationary period and the establishment of a mere expectancy of continued employment. It is this mere expectancy of continued employment that is recognized by the courts as property."

The Pennsylvania statewide Tenure Commission has made a series of statements as to what tenure should be (Hornbeck, 1977, p. 456):

> Tenure is not appropriately granted to a faculty member merely because he/she has done nothing wrong during the probationary period ... Second, every tenure decision is a statement by the institution about its future ... Third, the decision to grant or withhold tenure cannot be reached (ineluctably) from some litmus test ... Fourth, *it follows that participants in tenure decisions should be prepared to evaluate candidates in terms of institutional standards and goals.*

Community colleges are on the verge of allowing their own inactivity, policies, and procedures to provide their tenured faculty with the same type of "sanctuary for incompetent faculty" to which Nesbet refers. The author in his travels to both state and national conferences of college instructional administrators is continually amazed by the comments of other administrators which reveal a complete lack of evaluation procedures for tenured faculty members in their institutions. In some cases, student evaluation of faculty is "encouraged."

"Academic tenure is not a guarantee of a job for life short of disability or economic disaster," according to the National Commission on Higher Education Issues (Fleming, 1982, p. 10). They go on to say that "nothing will undermine the tenure system more completely than its being regarded as a system to protect faculty members from evaluations."

It must be pointed out that there will be some fairly sharp resistance to evaluation no matter what methods for evaluation purposes are introduced. Centra (1979, p. 1) points out that "a number of faculty members resist evaluation of teaching although most concede that some means must be found to prune the deadwood from their ranks." He says, "the resistance is based by faculty on two points: the classroom is their personal realm and any attempt to assess what happens behind classroom doors is an invasion of their privacy."

The two points of faculty resistance stated in the above paragraph are key "fallacy" points that are far too often accepted by administrators and believed by governing boards. This author contends that teaching can be evaluated and needs to be evaluated. Entrance into a faculty member's classroom for evaluation purposes is a necessary and positive move on behalf of those administrators who do not wish to merely "assume" that quality exists. Such an evaluation procedure is, of course, much stronger in terms of support when a faculty union or the majority of a faculty support "in-classroom" evaluation. Whether or not such faculty support is received prior to entering into an evaluation system, a fair system that recognizes both excellence in classroom instruction as well as identifies the "deadwood" of a faculty should prove itself valuable in the long-run. It should receive at least a quiet acceptance by those who are most concerned with the institution's reputation and quality instruction.

CONCERNS WITH STUDENT AND COLLEAGUE RATINGS

In his study of the research relative to student ratings of instructors, Centra (1979, pp. 152-153) concluded the following points: (1) students seem to rate elective courses or courses in the major area more highly than courses taken to fulfill a college requirement; (2) because students are generally lenient in their judgment, student ratings may be misleading about the effectiveness of some teachers. He supported the second point with a study by the Educational Testing Service (1975, p. 153) which pointed out that "only 12 percent of a national sample of almost 400,000 teachers received less than average ratings from students; the remainder were generally average, good, or excellent." Centra (p. 153) goes on to say that "the leniency in student ratings may, in fact, reinforce the inflated view held by some teachers about their teaching."

In regard to faculty feedback from students, Fraher (1982, pp. 123-124) points out some dangerous pitfalls or "hidden traps" in formal evaluations received by instructors. He says the "quantified *overall evaluation* given by students invariably reflects a higher opinion than an instructor might receive from his or her colleagues, or even from a self-evaluation. Students can be unforgiving in their attitudes toward teachers, but their formal, written evaluations tend to be generous." He continues by saying "students expect their teachers to be excellent; to rate a professor or tutor as 'good' may not be as complimentary as the teacher would like to think."

Caskin (1983, pp. 60-61) points out several defects in student ratings. There are areas, he notes, that students are not qualified to rate: students are not curriculum experts; they are not in a position to judge whether the instructor is knowledgeable in the field; they will not know if the course is as comprehensive as it should be. He also points to the inflexibility of student rating forms to accommodate a variety of teaching methods or approaches.

The research on evaluations by colleagues provides similar conclusions to the student ratings. Centra's (1979, p. 75) review of the research on "colleague evaluation" found that colleagues were generous in their ratings. They overwhelmingly evaluated overall instructor effectiveness as "excellent" or "good" (94 percent), which was even higher than student ratings. Also, colleague ratings were found to be not statistically reliable. The highest correlation found among ratings by different colleagues was about .26 for each item. Centra concludes that "this low reliability casts doubts on the value of colleague ratings as they were collected in this study." The above studies are most disturbing! Yet, such techniques provide the main sources of evaluation for many universities and colleges for both tenure and promotion purposes. Many community colleges and secondary schools have moved into use of student ratings as their primary source of evaluation. Centra says, "two year colleges use student ratings at least as much as the other two types of institutions" (p. 9). It becomes obvious that such information, while fairly easy to obtain and non-threatening for administrators to go after, may indeed present a poor decision-making tool for tenure and later evaluation decisions.

With the advent of more unionization and collective bargaining in the educational systems, faculty evaluation will play an ever more important role. Institutions using the "inflated" results of student ratings and low correlation ratings of colleagues will not assist governing boards and administrators in removing incompetent faculty for just cause reasons. It is also a fact that unionization leads to the support of faculty members who are evaluated negatively and are being considered for possible dismissal.

The literature is full of conflicting opinions about where teacher unions have stood on classroom evaluation. The following is an example of the conflict as summarized by McNeil (1981, p. 276):

> They hold that hiring and firing are the responsibility of the employer. In spite of their general opposition to negative assessment by school authorities, which they tend to view as deficient, leaders of some teacher organizations blame school boards and administrators for being irresponsible in hiring and evaluating incompetent teachers.

He goes on to point out that "these organizations *do not* take responsibility for removing incompetent teachers from the classroom" (p. 275).

It is in the light of such documented facts, relative to student and colleague ratings, that the author presents an administrative model evaluation system to consider for tenured faculty.

BOARD POLICY
ADMINISTRATIVE PROCEDURES

It was suggested in Chapter 4 that a board policy be established relative to evaluation:

Board Policy – Evaluation of Faculty, Assistants to Instruction, and Counselors: Tenured, Non-tenured and Part-time

It is the policy of the Board of Trustees that all faculty of the college shall be evaluated by their supervisors in order to assure that quality in instruction, other professional duties, and in professional conduct is maintained.

The following procedures for *tenured* faculty evaluation are proposed as a model to assist administrators in learning what to look for in both classroom and overall professional duty and conduct.

TENURED EVALUATIONS

Procedures for the Evaluation of All Full-Time Tenured Faculty, Assistants to Instruction, and Counselors

It is the responsibility of the college administration to implement the following procedures which will provide for the evaluation of *all tenured* faculty, assistants to instruction, and counselors:

1. The Division Chairpersons and Dean of Instruction (or his/her representative) will evaluate classes or labs of each tenured instructor and/or assistant to instruction in the college and complete the faculty evaluation form.

2. The Dean of Student Development will evaluate

counseling sessions, career workshops, classes or
seminars of tenured counselors.

3. The Division Chairpersons, Dean of Instruction (or
   his/her representative), or Dean of Student Development (for counselors) will also evaluate all other aspects
   of the jobs to be performed by faculty, assistants to
   instruction, and counselors. The criteria that will be used
   in the evaluation process in addition to classroom or
   other formal activity will include, where applicable:
   a. Advisory committee work in programs.
   b. Maintaining curriculum, course updates, and re-
      visions.
   c. College committee work.
   d. Maintaining records as required by law, college
      policy, and administrative regulations.
   e. Maintaining scheduled office hours.
   f. Attending and participating in faculty and division
      meetings.

4. A formal evaluation conference with the Division Chairperson, Dean of Instruction (or Dean of Student Development for counselors) and the faculty member will be
   held within a reasonable time period following a classroom visitation and/or evaluation filed on the other job
   performance criteria that are outlined above.

5. A faculty member, assistant to instruction, or counselor
   will be apprised of any defects and/or deficiencies in
   his/her performance as discovered in the formal evaluation process. The person evaluated will be advised to
   take appropriate action to remediate the defects/de-
   ficiencies cited.

6. All tenured faculty, assistants to instruction, and counselors will be formally evaluated a minimum of twice
   during any five-year period following election to tenure.

7. All evaluation visits will be made unannounced.

8. Faculty, assistants to instruction, and counselors who
   continue to display the same defects and deficiencies
   after several formal evaluations and conferences with
   appropriate administrators will be considered for more
   severe remediation steps.

9. A review of the defects and deficiencies cited by the Board of Trustees to the person affected will be conducted by the appropriate college Dean and other administrative persons involved.

The administrative evaluation should include the immediate administrative supervisor and other administrators charged with instructional responsibilities. Colleges need to review carefully the role of a department chairperson who may be voted in by faculty members or are included in the faculty senate or union. In short, department chairpersons need to be clearly identified as administrators if they are to be part of an administrative evaluation team.

Administrative evaluation responsibilities should rest in the hands of the professional administrators. Students and faculty are not charged with the hiring and/or dismissal responsibilities in community colleges. They are not trained or experienced in classroom evaluation techniques and it is unlikely they will establish patterns of defects and deficiencies, establish plans for improvement, follow-up with face-to-face evaluation, and place faculty on formal notices to remedy their defects and deficiencies. Exhibit 4 provides a comparison summary of types of evaluation systems.

SUMMARY

This chapter has attempted to build a case for an administrative classroom evaluation system for tenured faculty. The long-time sanctuary that tenure has provided for incompetent faculty at universities and colleges can easily provide the same *poor model* for the community college and secondary school systems in the United States and Canada.

Only when tenure is viewed as a means of continual employment for the competent, self-directed, professionally-oriented faculty will the mystique and misconceptions of tenure be removed.

In its summary on tenure and post-tenure evaluation, the National Commission on Higher Education Issues (Fleming, 1982, p. 9) stated:

> The Commission strongly affirms the continuing importance of faculty tenure as an essential instrument to

EXHIBIT 4

COMPARISON SUMMARY OF TYPES OF EVALUATION SYSTEMS

TYPE OF EVALUATION	OUTCOME ORIENTATION	ACCOUNTABILITY ROLE	QUALITY FACTORS
ADMINISTRATIVE EVALUATION	1. For Positive Reinforcement 2. For Identifying Improvement Needs 3. For Developing Remediation Processes	Professional Responsibility Require for All Faculty and Academic Support Personnel	Quality of Professional Administrators Experience Knowledge of Teaching/Learning Content Limitations
STUDENT ASSESSMENT OF INSTRUCTION	1. For Assessment of Major Strengths 2. For Student Input Into Weaknesses From a Learner's Viewpoint Only	Optional for Tenured Require for Non-Tenured for Personal Development Needs	Amateurs Non-Professional Assessment "Halo" Effect
"PEER" RULES IN EVALUATION	Content Improvement Centered	Optional or as Suggested by Administration; for Content Assessment and Improvement Suggestions in Content, Organization, and Depth	Non-Job Responsibilities Research Shows Strong Skew Toward Not Providing Negative Evaluation between Peers

protect academic freedom, and thereby ensure the highest quality in teaching and research.

But the time has come for campus administrations and faculties to review and, if needed, revise their procedures in order to assure themselves and the public that the procedures will produce fair, rigorous, and relevant evaluations.

The emphasis on *fair, rigorous, and relevant evaluations* points to the need for well-trained administrative evaluators to carry out such an important charge in the higher education institutions.

Weaknesses in student evaluation and peer evaluation systems were reviewed as to the inherent weaknesses which have been well documented. Neither system has proven to be useful in developing a strong and meaningful tenured faculty evaluation system.

A well-conceived classroom evaluation system conducted by competent and trained administrative personnel has been presented as a viable alternative to the other evaluation systems for educational institutions to consider. Paramount to the success of such a system is the experience and quality of administrators who will be doing the evaluations. Faculty support and understanding will be forthcoming only if the system proves to be fair, provides a due-process time period for correcting defects and deficiencies, and recognizes quality in those classrooms and for those teaching performances that warrant such recognition.

7

The Legal and Competency Needs of Academic Administrators

IT IS IMPORTANT TO NOTE that while many community colleges and secondary schools are focusing on phasing in faculty evaluation programs, very little has been done to strengthen the administrative evaluation competencies and legal knowledge of instructional vice presidents, deans of instruction, principals and/or department/ division chairpersons. Such neglect needs to be remedied if solid administrative evaluation systems are going to replace those systems which now feature a heavy emphasis on student, self, and peer evaluation. Perhaps fear, lack of confidence, lack of training, and lack of models of administrative evaluation create the willingness by administrators and governing boards to allow the weaker systems of evaluation to be introduced into college procedures and faculty negotiated contracts.

A study on the main developmental *needs* of department/division chairpersons' (Hammons and Wallace, 1977, pp. 62-66) summarized the following as the *highest-level needs* according to the "need categories" listed:

Indicated by % Age
of Respondents

Managerial Skills

Techniques of motivating faculty staff   72%

Staff/faculty evaluation   72%

Personnel Skills

Conducting performance appraisals   66%

**Skills Relating to Curriculum
& Instruction**

Evaluation of Instructor   73%

Miscellaneous Needs

The law and higher education   62%

The correlation between "the law and higher education" need and the evaluation skills needed by academic administrators is, undoubtedly, very high. Little formal training can be found in the backgrounds of most academic administrators that is related to the competencies needed for them to feel comfortable in their administrative-evaluation role. There is also very little information made available to most academic administrators to let them know how they will stand on the legal issues as they relate to faculty evaluation.

LEGAL SUPPORT FROM THE COURTS

Administrative evaluation of faculty and academic support personnel will uncover situations that are not tolerable for effective and proper management of the institution for its students. It is the administrator's job to identify such situations, properly discuss and document them, and work to have them remediated by the faculty members involved. After a reasonable period in the remediation process, movement toward termination of the individual(s) involved may be necessary. Lovain (1983, p. 419) identifies the personnel action necessary to terminate a tenured faculty member's employment for cause as "one of the most difficult that a college or university can take." He points to the disharmony that can occur within an institution after such action has been taken. Boards and administrators should be aware that incompetency is not an easy charge or basis on which to dismiss a faculty member for good cause. Piele (1981, p. 69) does point out, however, that "the use of expert testimony and performance evaluations in making determinations about school employee competence are slowly winning approval in courts." In an early edition of *The Yearbook of School Law,* (1980, p. 62) Piele pointed out that "the reason dismissals are overturned by the courts is the lack of defensible data based on *evaluations of performance* [emphasis added].

It is very possible to dismiss a tenured faculty member for cause. In doing so the school must be most careful to follow proper procedures. Lovain (1983, p. 419) points to the court records in recent years that have supported such administrative decisions. He says that "almost all recent challenges by tenured faculty to their dismissals for stated cause have been rejected by the courts, despite heightened legal protections of tenure." Such dismissals must, however, be supported by substantial evidence.

The four areas that provide grounds for most of the terminations are the following: (1) incompetence; (2) immorality; (3) neglect of duty; and (4) insubordination.

INCOMPETENCE (SUPPORT CASES)

The following is a summary of court cases that have supported administrative movement to terminate faculty for reasons of *incompetence.* Such cases break down the stereotype that tenure protects incompetent faculty from dismissals. These cases span a 10 to 12 year period:

In *Chung v. Park,*[1] a tenured professor was dismissed on grounds of intransigence in dealing with his supervisors, especially because of poor teaching. The federal district court held that the allegations were supported by substantial evidence.[2]

In *Jarva v. Fayetteville University,*[3] a tenured professor was dismissed for, *inter alia,* poor teaching, being unprepared for classes, and poor relations with students. His civil rights

94 Evaluating for Excellence

challenge to the dismissal was rejected by the court.[4]

The Missouri Supreme Court considered the dismissal of a tenured junior college professor for incompetency, inefficiency, and insubordination in *Saunders v. Reorganized School District No. 2 of Osage County.*[5] The court upheld the dismissal and held that the charge of inefficiency was supported by evidence of the plaintiff's manner of teaching.[6]

The above cases were summarized by Lovain (1983-84, pp. 422-423). Lovain points out that the cases show "the courts will defer to the expertise of academic administrators" when charges of incompetence in teaching "are supported by substantial and relevant evidence" (p. 423). The following two cases relate to incompetence as documented by administrative classroom evaluations:

A local school board's decision to terminate a tenured teacher was sustained by the Supreme Court of Minnesota on the basis that substantial evidence of unfitness to teach, particularly evidence of lack of student progress, was supported in the administrative hearing record. The teacher had served for nineteen consecutive years in the school district, but had received previous notices of teaching deficiencies, including lack of rapport with students, poor communication with parents, failure to follow adopted school board lesson plans and irrational grading of students. Six classroom observations were undertaken over a five-month period and the teacher was regularly appraised of his deficiencies. In reviewing the entire record, the high court found that substantial evidence supported four major teaching deficiencies: (1) excessive use of worksheets, (2) lack of rapport, (3) lack of appropriate student discipline, and (4) lack of student progress. The latter basis, lack of student progress, was specifically related to express statutory grounds for discharge under Minnesota law.[7]

A case from Illinois illustrates the dimensions of effective evaluation when applied to a dismissal for negligent failure to supervise and instruct students. A tenured elementary school teacher was dismissed following parental complaints and classroom observations that consistently confirmed her inability to maintain classroom order or adequately prepare for subject matter discussion. Following initial complaints by parents and negative evaluations by the school principal, the teacher was informed by the school board of her specific deficiencies in teaching performance and provided with opportunities during the ensuing school year to improve. In the second year she was periodically observed by the principal and three other faculty members, all of whom evaluated the teacher's understanding of the subject matter and control over students as unsatisfactory. Sixty-four days of remediation were permitted, but no correction of deficiencies was noted by observers. In affirming dismissal, the appellate court noted that the teacher's deficiencies were long standing and represented fundamental teaching inadequacies. The notice provided was appropriate and the period of remediation was reasonable for correction of the deficiencies. The court's reliance on classroom observation reports completed by teachers and the principal illustrates the considerable weight courts give to the evidentiary value of these records.[8]

The above two cases were summarized by Piele (1983, p. 53). The following case, summarized in 1983 (Piele, p. 54), allowed other factors beyond classroom evaluation to be included in an employment decision.

Lack of strict compliance with New Jersey statute law requiring classroom evaluations would not bar a school board from considering other factors relevant to teaching competency in determining to nonrenew a non-tenured teacher. In affirming the nonrenewal, the local board's right to base its employment decision on a broad base of input from a variety of people, including students, parents and members of the public as well as a board member whose child was instructed by the teacher was sustained.[9]

In 1980, the following two cases were summarized by Piele (p. 63). He summarized the third case in his 1978 Yearbook (pp. 74-75).

Illinois statutes require certain dismissal procedures to be followed.

In December, 1976, the school board directed that a teacher be served with a notice of deficiencies. The following March the board gave the teacher a notice of charges and its intention to seek her dismissal. The board alleged that the teacher failed to correct deficiencies, failed to follow instruction of her supervisors, and had a pattern of deficiency with respect to lapses in student discipline and lesson planning and presentation. A subsequent hearing was conducted by a hearing officer who held for the teacher. The board's appeal to the circuit court resulted in a reversal. However, the appellate court ruled that although the lower court had correctly determined that the hearing officer had imposed the incorrect burden of proof on the board, it erred in remanding the case back to the hearing officer for a new determination.[10]

Maryland's highest state court sustained the discharge
of a teacher for incompetency.[11] The specific charges that
the school principal listed included (1) inability to manage
her class, (2) poor preparation, (3) improper attitude toward
pupils, and (4) inability to relate. Procedural irregularities
occurred during that administrative review process; however,
the court held that the denial of a proper administrative
hearing was cured by judicial review.

The Fourth Circuit Court in a civil rights action considered a teacher's allegation that the evaluation form used
violated her Fourteenth Amendment equal protection
rights.[12] The board had decided not to renew her contract
on grounds of incompetency based on the principal's negative
recommendation and the evaluation form. The teacher
charged that since the form, a checklist of desirable characteristics, had not been validated for job-relatedness, it
created an impermissible classification of all teachers deemed
incompetent. Rejecting this argument, the court found no
evidence that the use of the form "disproportionally affected
members of any identifiable group."[13] The court went on
to say: ". . . an evaluation of teacher competence is necessarily
a highly subjective determination that does not lend itself
to precise quantification, nor, we might add, to judicial review.
It is an area in which school officials must remain free to
exercise their judgment and discretion . . ."[14]

Two cases in 1981 were decided in behalf of the board
based upon in-class evaluations by their administrators. In
both cases, described below, attempts at remedy by the
administration were not followed by the faculty member
involved (Piele, pp. 69-70):

In a South Dakota case, a teacher whose contract was
not renewed on the basis that she was incompetent challenged
the evaluation of her teaching performance on the grounds
that the evaluations were insufficient to meet the requisite
standard of substantial evidence. The teacher was formally
evaluated each of the three years she taught in the school
system. In each year she was criticized for her method of
structional organization. Several suggestions to improve her
organizational deficiencies were given. On three occasions the
teacher was criticized in her evaluations for failing to maintain classroom order in allowing students to randomly leave
their seats without permission and place their feet on the
desks. On her first evaluation she was told that improvement
in classroom atmosphere would result in greater interest and
better attitudes in her students. The teacher's last evaluation

in March of 1977, rated her unsatisfactory in regard to these criticisms. Her own testimony reflected that she did not take the suggested corrective measures but willfully refused to comply, stating that her methods of teaching were better. The board's determinations were based on satisfactory performance in the following areas: (1) creating an appropriate classroom atmosphere; (2) developing student interest and attitudes; and (3) possessing and demonstrating positive qualities of organization. These determinations were evidenced in a large part by the teacher's evaluation forms. These evaluations were prepared by the principal of the school in the course of observing the teacher's classroom teaching performances. The Supreme Court of South Dakota found that the evaluations were sufficient to support a charge of incompetence and affirmed the school board's action in refusing to renew the teacher's contract.[15]

Two decisions from the Iowa Supreme Court involved school board dismissals based on incompetency. In both instances, the school employee manifested symptoms of psychological stress that were a factor in the board's determination. In one case, a school board sought to dismiss a teacher based on charges of inadequate maintenance of discipline during class, excessive and ineffective use of films, ineffective classroom teaching, and failure to improve and cooperate with the school administrators who tried to assist in correcting deficiencies. The board heard fourteen hours of testimony in the termination hearing. The teacher appealed to an adjudicator who reversed the board's decision. The board then appealed to the district court where the adjudicator's decision was affirmed. The Iowa Supreme Court found the adjudicator's decision was unsupported by a preponderance of the competent evidence in the record when that record was viewed as whole and that there was "just cause" for termination. The teacher contended he was entitled to be considered an ill teacher, but the court determined incompetence was not due to any physical or mental disability. The judgment of the district court and the decision of the adjudicator were reversed and the board's termination decision was reinstated.[16]

In another case summarized by Piele (1975, p. 166), a notice to remedy defects had been sent to the teacher:

A series of events followed from a board's dissatisfaction with the professional performance of a tenured teacher on indefinite contract in Missouri. The teacher was informed of such dissatisfaction by formal evaluations and conferences. Notice of failure to improve was sent by registered mail, warning the teacher that certain defined deficiencies must be corrected for continued employment. The following year the teacher was transferred to another school to work under a principal who was familiar with her problems. Officials felt that her performance did not improve during the second year and the board terminated the teacher's contract. The Missouri Court of Appeals reversed the lower court action that had reversed the board action, and remanded, reasoning that the board's action was supported by substantial evidence and that due process was used in an effort to improve performance following the procedure specified in the tenure act.[17]

The following cases point out incompetence in the classroom as documented by administrative evaluation:

Missouri statutes contain a numbered listing of grounds for terminating a permanent teacher in which incompetency, inefficiency, and insubordination are grouped together under a single number.[18] Usually charges are stated in such a way as to reflect each of these three causes. For example, the warning sent to a tenured teacher, after an unsuccessful attempt to improve her performance, alluded to failure to provide properly for learning needs of students, complete inability to maintain discipline, and failure to follow administrative direction. The teacher did not contest the sufficiency of evidence but contended that the board failed to follow statutory procedures in dismissing her. The courts held for the board.[19]

A discharged tenured teacher in Louisiana sued the school board maintaining that it had not substantiated the charges of incompetency against her. The court disagreed, referring to the 236-page hearing transcript and noting also that the teacher was the only witness in her own defense. Not until the end of the hearing did her attorney raise a question of untimely notice. The court also rejected this challenge.

Where a tenured junior college teacher was discharged, the Supreme Court of Missouri ruled that there was sufficient evidence to support the board's finding that the teacher had been guilty of inefficiency and insubordination. The court further ruled that none of the teacher's rights had been violated.[20]

A Pennsylvania teacher was under a temporary employee contract teaching art during 1970-71. After seven observation reviews in one year, he received as many unsatisfactory ratings from his department head. Based upon these evaluations, the teacher was terminated at the end of his contract, June, 1972, after exercising his right to a board hearing. The commonwealth court affirmed the trial court, noting that the hearing record presented evidence that the teacher's lessons were not taught in accordance with lesson plans, that classroom time was poorly budgeted, that presentations were confused, and that the teacher was unwilling to make necessary adjustments.[21]

The four cases above were summarized by Piele (1978, p. 76).

NEGLECT OF DUTY (SUPPORT CASES)

The neglect of duty cases center on disobedience of the college or other institution rules, missing of classes, office hours, etc.

Some cases, which have been supported by the courts, that relate to faculty dismissal for neglect of duties beyond the classroom follow:

In *Jawa*, the court cited the plaintiff's failure to keep office hours and properly advise his students, and his unwillingness to follow proper procedures as valid grounds for his discharge.[22]

In *Bates v. Sponberg*,[23] a tenured professor was dismissed in part for failing to submit required reports on the project he directed.

Missed classes have also been held to be valid evidence of adequate cause for discharge where one tenured professor refused to teach an assigned class[24] and another took a leave of absence he had been forbidden to take.[25]

In two cases, tenured faculty lost their jobs after failing to appear for work at the appointed time.[26] In both cases, the courts held that the faculty had thereby voluntarily abandoned their property interests in continued employment.[27]

The above cases were summarized by Lovain (pp. 425-426).

Faculty can be discharged for neglect of their duties beyond their teaching duties. These duties include (1) attending faculty workshops, (2) the keeping of office hours, (3) filing required reports and agreements, and (4) institutional committee work (Lovain, 1983-84, p. 426).

INSUBORDINATION (SUPPORT CASES)

Lower courts have supported colleges and universities as having the right to expect their faculty to work "cooperatively and harmoniously with their colleagues and administrators" (Lovain, 1983-84, p. 428). He cites the following cases in support of this contention:

> Thus, certain legitimate state interests may limit the right of a public employee, specifically the right of a state university professor, to say and do what he pleases: for example (1) the need to maintain discipline and harmony among co-workers; (2) the need for confidentiality; (3) the need to curtail conduct which impedes the teacher's proper and competent performance of his daily duties; (4) the need to encourage a close and personal relationship between the employee and his superiors, when that relationship calls for loyalty and confidence; (5) the need to maintain a competition of different views in the classroom and to prevent the use of the classroom by a teacher deliberately to proselytize for a certain cause or knowingly to emphasize only that selection of data best conforming to his own personal biases; (6) the need to prevent activities disruptive of the educational process and to provide for the orderly functioning of the university.[28]

In *Stasny v. Board of Trustees,*[29] a tenured professor with a history of unapproved absences was denied permission to take a leave of absence. The University threatened him with disciplinary action if he defied their decision, but he took the leave anyway. He was dismissed for, *inter alia* insubordination, but asserted in court that (1) his defiance was merely a single respectful act of disobedience," not insubordination; and (2) his dismissal violated his right to academic freedom and freedom of expression.[30] The court rejected these arguments, observing that "academic freedom is not a license for activity at variance with job related procedures and requirements, nor does it encompass activities which are internally destructive to the proper function of the university or disruptive to the education process."[31]

The above cases were summarized by Lovain (pp. 428-430). Insubordination can take various forms as outlined by Piele in the next several cases.

> The Pennsylvania CommonwealthCourt reversed a reinstatement order of the Pennsylvania Secretary of Education and held that a teacher's actions warranted dismissal for insubordination. The facts disclosed that the teacher had submitted lesson plans that were incomplete and not in conformity with the format for lesson plans contained in a bulletin and policy manual concerning such plans, failed to report for cafeteria duty as instructed by the assistant

principal and became verbally hostile and argumentative when he was requested to teach a second period class due to the illness of another teacher, refused to sign a note relative to his claim of illness and became abusive, and failed to keep a grade book in accordance with requirements of the district.[32]

After a long series of incidents, a tenured music teacher in Massachusetts was charged with "insubordination, or other good cause." Problems began when he bypassed the administration and went directly to the school committee. This conduct continued even after warnings. The following year, he issued a memorandum ridiculing the principal and the faculty curriculum committee. When he was denied a pay raise he lobbied the school committee to reverse its decision. Subsequently, he threatened a work stoppage as band director and refused to return his contract even after several requests from the superintendent. In bringing this action, the employee charged that in discharging him the board violated the collective bargaining agreement. The court disagreed, sustaining the board's decision.[33]

In North Carolina, the state supreme court held that the refusal of a teacher to sign a statement of deficiencies was inadequate grounds for discharge.[34]. However, a state appellate court sustained the dismissal of a probationary teacher for insubordination in connection with the use of corporal punishment.[35] The court held that the evidence warranted the findings, the procedures were proper, and the board's corporal punishment policy did not violate statutory provisions permitting its use (Piele, 1981, pp. 64-65).

A Delaware federal district court overturned the discharge of a tenured music teacher for "willful and persistent insubordination."[36] An apparent personality conflict between the two led to unsatisfactory ratings by the principal who recommended discharge when the teacher criticized the administration. The court determined that the discharge was for constitutionally impermissable reasons and ordered reinstatement, damages, and other relief requested (Piele, 1980, p. 59).

The reason given for the dismissal of a vocational education teacher from a state school in Kentucky was "friction" between her and her superior. The teacher challenged the termination, maintaining that a state statute required the state board of education to grant approval before such employees could be dismissed. After rejecting her claim of statutory and constitutional violations, the state supreme court observed that sufficient evidence showed that she was uncooperative and insubordinate to her superiors.[37] (Piele, 1978, p. 66).

SUMMARY

The needs of educational administrators appear high in the areas of *evaluation, performance appraisals, motivating faculty,* and the *law as it applies to higher education.* Academic administrators have gained support in the courts in recent years. Such support for terminating tenured faculty should destroy the *myth* that tenure makes it impossible to dismiss faculty.

While the courts have acknowledged tenure to be a property interest of a faculty position—with the assurance that dismissal procedures must conform to the requirements of due process—they have also affirmed with consistency that colleges and secondary schools can terminate faculty for adequate cause. They have, however, affirmed such cases only where they have found that proper procedures were followed.

Lovain points out the Supreme Court has stated that "it is not the role of the federal courts to set aside decisions of school administrators which the court may view as lacking in wisdom or compassion."[38] He adds another case to support fact finding which "when reached by correct procedures and supported by substantial evidence, are entitled to great weight, and the court should never lightly substitute its judgment for that of the board."[39]

The *New York Institute of Technology v. State Division of Human Rights* case produced the following statement in support of management's responsibility in personnel decisions:

> The management of the university is primarily the responsibility of those equipped with the special skills and sensitivities necessary for so delicate a task. One of the most sensitive functions of the university administration is the appointment, promotion, and retention of the faculty. It is for this reason that the courts, and administrative agencies as well, should "only rarely assume academic oversight, except with the greatest caution and restraint, in such sensitive areas as faculty appointment, promotion, and tenure, especially in institutions of higher learning"[40] (Lovain, 1983, p. 433).

In his summary, Lovain points out that "the judiciary has shown considerable deference to the expertise of academic administrators in personnel decisions. They acknowledge that dismissals of tenured postsecondary faculty are within the competence, as well as the power, of college and university administrators, and, unless arbitrary or capricious, such decisions should remain there" (p. 433). This chapter was developed to give governing boards and academic administrators a look at two major factors in evaluating faculty. The first factor is the need of academic administrators to obtain adequate support and training relative to faculty and staff evaluation. The second is to show that courts do indeed support competent and sensitive evaluation reports by administrators which lead to terminations of faculty. In *none* of the cases cited did any peer, self, or student evaluations in conflict with the administrative evaluations appear. The courts, as pointed out by Lovain and others, lean to the expertise of academic administrators in personnel decisions. The question must be asked, "Why have some boards and administrators allowed their *expertise and responsibilities* to be delegated to students, faculty peers, and 'self' in negotiated collective bargaining contracts or non-negotiated evaluation systems?"

CHAPTER 7 ENDNOTES

[1]377F. Supp. 218 (M.D. Pa. 1974).

[2]Id. at 530.

[3]426F. Supp. 218 (E.D.N.C. 1976).

[4]Id. at 230.

[5]520 S.W. 2d 29 (Mo. 1975).

[6]Id. at 33.

[7]Whaley v. Anoka-Hennepin Indep. School Dist., 325 N.W.2d 128 (Minn. 1982).

[8]Community Unit School Dist. v. Maclin, 435 N.E.2d 845 (Ill. 1982).

[9]Dore v. Bedminster Twp. Bd. of Educ., 449 A.2d 547 (N.J. Super. 1982)

[10]Board of Educ. of Minooka Commun. Consol. School Dist. v. Ingles, 394 N.E.2d 69 (Ill. App. Ct. 1979).

[11]Board of Educ. of Charles Cty. v. Crawford, 395 A.2d 835 (Md. 1979). See also Gargiul v. Board of Educ. of the Liverpool Cent. School Dist., 416 N.Y.S.2d 119 (app. Div. 1979); Lowe v. Board of Educ. of City of Chicago, 395 N.E.2d 59 (Ill. App. Ct. 1979).

[12]Beauchamp v. Davis, 550 F.2d 959 (4th Cir. 1977).

[13]Id. at 961.

[14]Id.

[15]Busker v. Board of Educ. of Elk Point, 295 N.W.2d 1 (S.D. 1980). See also Linfield v. Nyquist, 401 N.E.2d 909 (N.Y. 1980, where the penalty for incompetency, dismissal from the entire New York City school system, was not deemed excessive.

[16]Board of Dirs. of Sioux City v. Mroz, 295 N.W.2d 447 (Iowa 1980).

[17]Meredith v. Board of Educ., 513 S.W.2d 740 (Mo. App. 1974).

[18]Moore v. Board of Educ. of Sp. School Dist. of St. Louis Cty., 547 S.W.2d 188 (Mo. App. 1977).

[19]Cook v. Natchitoches Parish School Dist., 342 So. 2d 702 (La. App. 1977).

[20]Saunders v. Reorganized School Dist. No. 2 of Osage Cty., 420 S.W.2d 29 (Mo. 1975).

[21]Hickey v. Board of School Directors of Pennsylvania Manor School, 328 A.2d 549 (Pa. Cmwlth, 1974).

[22]426 F. Supp. at 224.

[23]547 F.2d 325 (6th Cir. 1976).

[24]Smith v. Kent State University, 696 F.2d 476, 479 (6th Cir. 1983).

[25]Trustees of Central Wash. Univ., 32 Wash. App. 239, 647 P.2d 496, 506-07 (1982).

[26]Kalme v. West Virginia Board of Regents, 539 F.2d 1346 (4th Cir. 1976); Akyeampong v. Coppin State College, 538 F. Supp. 986 (D. Md. 1982).

[27]Kalme, 539 F.2d at 1348; Akyeampong, 530 F. Supp. at 990.

[28]Keddie, 412 F. Supp. at 1271.

[29]Stastny v. Board of Trustees of Central Washington Univ., 32 Wash. App. 239, 647 P.2d 496 (1982).

[30]647 P.2d at 502-03.

[31]647 P.2d at 504.

[32]Clairton School Dist. v. Strinich, 413 A.2d 26 (Pa. Commw. Ct. 1980).

[33]Lower v. North Middlesex Reg. School Comm., 395 N.W.2d 1310 (Mass. App. 1979)

[34]Hasty v. Bellamy, 260 S.E.2d 135 (N.C. 1979).

[35]Kurtz v. Winston-Salem Forsyth Cty. Bd. of Educ., 250 S.E. 2d 718 (N.C. Ct. App. 1979).

[36]Eckerd v. Indian River School Dist., 475 F. Supp. 1350 (D. Del. 1979).

[37]Wagner v. Department of Educ. State Personnel Bd., 549 S.W.2d 300 (Ky. 1977).

[38]Wood v. Strickland, 420 U.S. 308, 326 (1975).

[39]Duke, *supra* note 86, at 859; *see* Saunders, *supra* note 39, at 35.

[40]New York Inst. of Technology v. State Division of Human Rights, 40 N.Y. 2d 598, 353 N.E.2d 598, 386 N.Y.S. 2d 685, 688 (1976), (quoting Matter of Pace Coll. v. Commission of Human Rights of City of N.Y., 38 N.Y. 2d, 28, 339 N.E.2d 880, 377 N.Y.S.2d 471, 478 (1975).

8

*". . . such evaluation can reinforce
personal growth and instructional improvement
throughout a faculty member's career . . ."*
Bevan, 1980

Guiding the Evaluator: Positive Evaluations

THE NUMBER ONE JOB of instructional administrators should be evaluating faculty who are performing their teaching and other job responsibilities with a high degree of competence and enthusiasm.

In a tenured faculty, thoroughly screened during both the hiring and non-tenured evaluation processes, the large majority of administrative evaluations should result in positive written and oral evaluation reports. They may be sprinkled with suggested improvements but seldom reach the level of *remediation suggestions* that will be discussed in chapters 8, 9 and 10.

This chapter will focus on positive evaluation statements that evaluators may make on those areas of instruction that are outlined in the classroom evaluation form suggested in chapter 5. The other job responsibilities should also receive positive evaluation statements when they are being competently carried out. Such evaluation reinforces the importance of these job responsibilities and also sharpens the evaluation responsibilities of those administrators involved with faculty and academic support personnel. Some of these areas of a faculty member's job performance go completely neglected by those colleges that rely solely on a student evaluation system.

This author takes the stance that it is most important that *all faculty be evaluated* so they know how they stand in an institution. The need for recognition and the knowledge that "someone cares enough to check on my work" is a prime motivator for many persons. Competent faculty and academic support persons will often go out of their way to share some of the exciting and highly motivating things they are doing in their classroom or in other job functions. The motivation that is stimulated through positive reinforcement and recognition is hard to measure but is so important in meeting persons' higher-level needs. This will be discussed in more detail in chapter 9 which deals with "Rewarding Excellence in Instruction."

Bevan (1980, p. 3) raises a good analogy relative to college professors who see the ends of an evaluation process as punitive and/or an infringement to their privacy. He considers such a posture as "strange" for these professors "who daily devote their time to developing critical skills and forming thought and judgment in others, who regularly and systematically gauge the process of these evolving processes, and who regard constructive judgment as a work of a professional academician."

The next few pages will provide some *examples of positive evaluation statements* by administrators relating to the various in-class dynamics that take place. There also can be found positive evaluation statements relative to other professional responsibilities at the end of the in-class evaluation section.

EVALUATION QUESTIONS FROM THE EVALUATION FORM FOR FACULTY, ASSISTANTS TO INSTRUCTION, AND COUNSELORS

Question 1:

What evidence is there that the person *is* or *is not* prepared for this class, lab, or counseling activity?

a. The instructor was organized and had good notes to refer

to for his presentation.
b. The instructor was well prepared in this seminar to review the lab assignment, questions from the textbook, and lecture questions her students came with.
c. This instructor presented a well organized, logical, enthusiastic lecture. He presented his lecture with *no reference* to notes, used outside references, and allowed students to question him.

Question 2:

Is there evidence that there is appropriate homework, class participation, and other expectations of the students?
a. Students looked up to hear the lecture but yet took comprehensive notes.
b. The short quiz at the start of the class is a good motivator for students to review their notes and text assignment before coming to class.
c. Students had prepared the assigned exercises and responded well to questions from the teacher.

Question 3:

Does the person use good teaching/counseling techniques and provide a good learning environment.
a. Yes. Notes were available but used only as guide. The use of examples illustrates her years of experience in the field.
b. The presentation had structure and logical sequence and it was given in a relaxed, yet well paced manner. He knew exactly what he wanted to accomplish and how he wanted to accomplish it.
c. Her enthusiasm is a definite asset to her methods of presentation.

Question 4:

Does the person demonstrate *adequate knowledge* of the subject, activity, or skill?
a. I commend this instructor for acknowledging articles, books, and other sources which will be helpful to strengthen the students' understanding of today's topic.
b. Yes. She is spontaneous and knowledgeable in reviewing

the correct answers on the test she passed back.
c. The lecture was presented in scientific terms, very informative and well illustrated with examples. The terminology was appropriately used and adequate for the class.

Question 5:

Is the discussion or activity germane to the *course syllabus?*
a. Yes. Ocean currents is an important topic in the area of the course syllabi dealing with the "earth's atmosphere and world climate."
b. Yes. The muscular-skeletal system is included in the course syllabus.

Question 6:

What evidence is there that the *course syllabus* will be completed as required?
a. The instructor's outline showed the class to be on chapter 12 at this time. The evaluator found this to be the case.
b. An end-of-semester comprehensive exam will be given in all the beginning accounting courses. This instructor is progressing on schedule.
c. This course must go through the Civil War and Reconstruction. He is well into the Civil War with two full weeks of lecture to go.

Question 7:

Does the person evaluate student progress on a regular basis?
a. Yes, a test was announced for Monday. This is the second test (mid-term) and will cover chapters 5, 6 and 7.
b. Excellent! Students came in early to discuss the material with the instructor; she calls on them by name and knows them well enough to know how and what to ask certain students in order to gain their responses.

Question 8:

Was sound use of testing and review techniques used where appropriate?

a. This instructor began the class by distributing and reviewing completed tests. She also placed the grading system for the test on the board.
b. Questioning, a short quiz and review of the quiz, and a review of a handout for an announced test were all used during this class period.

Question 9:

Are grading standards observed to be at a level expected for college?

a. The instructor's grading curve appears to be in line with her students' success on the standardized end-of-semester exam.
b. His engineering students obtain very similar grades at universities after transfer. He is complimented by his colleagues at these colleges.

Question 10:

Does the person have meaningful interaction with the students?

a. Student interaction was used very effectively. The instructor allows relevant student responses throughout her lecture. Many of their responses brought out personal or family related examples.
b. Respect for the instructor was evident by the response to questions, note taking, and high degree of "listening" that appeared to be taking place.

Question 11:

How has the person encouraged student participation in the class?

a. Students were asked questions, readily responded, and were encouraged to add personal examples to the parts of the lecture they were most familiar with.
b. The instructor was well prepared. Students had been given a lecture guide during the Wednesday class, which was used to prepare them for today's lecture (excellent stimulus tool).

Question 12:

Is the person able "to get materials across" and to answer student questions clearly?

a. Lecture, with questions, role playing, and interesting examples kept the class moving with high student interest.

b. Use of facial and body moves were used by the instructor for illustration of types of non-verbal communications.

Question 13:

Does the person use appropriate audio-visual materials in the classroom/activity?

a. Audio-visual support was used to help pace the lecture. Summary statements and terms were projected on the screen to aid in the introduction of lecture points.

b. She made excellent use of her maps and the overhead projector.

OTHER PROFESSIONAL RESPONSIBILITIES

Question 1:

Does the person maintain attendance records as required by the college and state?

a. He expressed his distaste of students not being present and coming in late. This is a good way to let them know he values attendance.

b. The instructor shared her grading policy, attendance policy, and the objectives that she shares with her students with me. They are comprehensive and clear.

Question 2:

Does the person attend and participate in faculty meetings, division meetings, and college committees?

a. He has served will on the curriculum committee and made suggestions that were well received and implemented.

b. This instructor is to be congratulated for the many contributions he has made to the curriculum committee, campus research projects, and to his fellow instructors in new course preparation.

Question 3:

˙Does the person maintain required office hours?
a. He encouraged students to seek his help during his posted office hours.
b. Students are required to hold individual conference hours during the instructor's office hours.

Question 4:

Does the person keep current on the latest developments in his/her field of study?
a. This instructor is to be complimented on her recent selection to the National Science Foundation summer program on Ethics in Nursing.
b. This instructor is complimented on his professional activities in the state Geographical Society. He is past president and ran a high quality meeting a year ago for his colleagues on our campus.

Question 5:

Does the person exhibit a positive working relationship with colleagues and the administration?
a. This instructor is the one I always turn to for assistance in budgets, schedules, and curriculum revisions in her department. She is always willing to teach evening classes and to work at the prison each year.
b. She is very open to suggestions and is a positive influence on campus.

Question 6:

Does the person keep course syllabi, college and state reports updated and completed on time?
a. He does a fine job in the classroom and an equally fine job in anything I have asked him to do: curriculum development, textbook selection, or whatever.
b. Her leadership in updating six course syllabi this year was outstanding. We are now ready for the state board review.

SUMMARY

It is easy for the reader to get caught up in the very positive evaluations that have been presented on the preceding pages. The examples given were spread out over the many questions and dynamic areas that can be evaluated in both in-class and other areas of job responsibility. The questions relate to the sample comprehensive administrative evaluation form presented in chapter 5.

In discussing faculty development, Bevan (1980, p. 3) says, "It is recognized that *faculty evaluation* can be an important aspect of faculty development." The reason he believes so is because, "such evaluation can reinforce personal growth and instructional improvement throughout a faculty member's career. In one sense," he goes on to say, "the primary goals of faculty evaluation are identical to those of faculty development, i.e., the improvement of college teaching and the improvement of student learning (p. 3)."

Positive evaluations are just as necessary for the average to superior faculty and academic support personnel as negative evaluation is for the below average or incompetent instructor. Positive evaluation lets a competent instructor know how he or she stands in the eyes of the institution. It can provide a very strong sense of motivation for continuing improvements and excellence in instruction. It also provides for the higher-level needs of faculty and others that basic salary and job security do not satisfy.

Positive evaluation is a necessary part of a comprehensive administrative evaluation system. It provides the balance that is necessary when some faculty are receiving negative evaluations. It places charges of arbitrary, capricious, and discriminatory practices in proper perspective. A faculty union and individual faculty members will see that the negative evaluations are in the minority.

The faculty receiving positive evaluations should represent the "dog," and those who will be negatively evaluated should represent the "tail" in any community college or secondary school. Seeing how much dog the tail can wag will be a true test of a comprehensive and effective administrative evaluation system that purports to be fair and objective.

9

"... faculty evaluation ought not to
be endorsed or implemented if there
is little or no intent to support
developmental efforts."

Bevan, 1980

Rewarding Excellence in Instruction

PRESIDENT RONALD REAGAN raised many different responses to his suggestion during the summer of 1983 that teachers should be given "merit increases" for superior teaching performances. Immediate reactions from the National Education Association (NEA) and the American Federation of Teachers were negative to the President's suggestion. Both organizations pointed out the inequities that exist in all teacher salaries, and they identified salary as an overriding concern prior to schools getting into merit pay. The governors in the states of Tennessee, Florida, California, Virginia, and Oklahoma have since pushed to create legislation to support merit pay increases for faculty.

The 98th Congress of the United States commissioned a "Merit Pay Task Force" to develop a posture for merit pay from the federal level. The study was chaired by Congressman Paul Simon of Illinois. The first major issue addressed by the task force was that of the very low pay of teachers throughout the United States. The well balanced committee was given representation from the AFT president, Albert Shanker, and Mary Hatwood Futrell, president of the National Education Association.

The committee described merit pay as a system that rewards exemplary teaching by either a bonus or an increased annual salary. Simon's committee indicates that merit pay defines the reward for performance in dollar terms, although this could include sabbaticals, tuition assistance or other bonuses (Perkins, p. 5). They also caution schools that in the development of criteria and procedures dealing with merit pay, abuses need to be avoided "that would grant rewards for reasons other than outstanding teacher performance" (p. 7).

In *Newsweek's* Gallup Poll during June of 1983, 80 percent of the respondents were in favor of "basing teachers' salaries on merit to attract and retain better public-school teachers."

Sbaratta (1983, p. 27) suggests that while encouraging persons to obtain excellence may be the most critical task, the rewarding of excellent in performance is "the trickiest." He states that "encouraging excellence in teaching is the academic dean's most critical task."

It is the contention of Andrews and Marzano (1983) that a recognition process should evolve out of a strong, objective evaluation system. They point out that the average faculty member can control, weaken, or destroy highly motivated faculty if the *group process* is allowed to operate in a climate that is void of a recognition process. The goal of such a merit recognition system is a "positive skewing" of teacher performance to the right hand side of a *normal curve* (see Exhibit 5).

Exhibit 5

Intended Outcome of Faculty
Merit System: A "Positive Skewing"
of Teacher Performance.

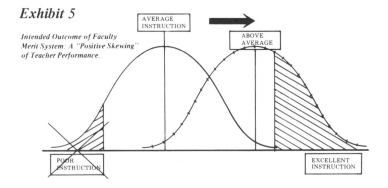

Bevan (1980, p. 3) summarizes the need for faculty evaluation as follows:

> Because faculty members are a college's or university's primary resource for stimulating learning and the central force in maintaining and enhancing its character and vitality, programs of faculty evaluation and faculty development should be of highest priority and appropriate reward systems should be established to reinforce them.

DEVELOPING A PHILOSOPHICAL BASIS FOR MERIT

The philosophical basis for a merit system should be identified by each community college considering such a system. The movement into merit pay by state and federal legislators and governors may be done for political expediency reasons. Such efforts may be rushed and highly resented by persons who are to administer the program or legislation as well as the faculty and/or other recipients of the system.

Maslow's needs-heirarchy theory pointed out that, before one if ready to satisfy higher-level needs, they must feel a certain satisfaction level and security in their basic needs. Adequate pay for teachers would be an example of a basic survival need. It must be adequate enough to "secure the essentials of living."

Herzberg (1966), in his "Motivation-Hygiene" theory, proposes (1) pay, (2) working conditions, (3) relations with co-workers, (4) competence of supervisors, and (5) company policies as "hygiene" factors present in work situations. These factors are very similar to Maslow's lower-level needs. According to Herzberg, these must be met in an adequate manner if worker dissatisfaction is to be avoided. Steinmetz (1978) recognized the similar aspects of both theories. He saw them both as proposing a two-step approach — meeting necessary "hygiene" factors or lower-level needs (step 1), and then higher-level needs such as self esteem (step 2).

Faculty merit pay and/or recognition systems should be seen as attempts by community colleges and other education systems to provide esteem or recognition as an important motivational factor (higher level) according to Andrews and

Marzano (1984). They do, however, point out the need for those institutions to *first provide* for adequate hygiene factors. They also point out that such reward systems should "evolve from hard work and exceptional efforts" on the part of *individual* faculty. This is where the strength of an administrative evaluation system is tested. A fair, objective, and effective system for evaluating job performance criteria that is agreed upon by key parties within an institution must be developed (Cheshire and Hagameyer, 1981). Selden (1978, p. 32) points out that the reward to be given should be stipulated. How many may qualify—from one faculty member per division to a variable number, or all who meet the criteria within a given time frame—should be determined.

THE RESEARCH ON MERIT

In its "Research Action Brief" on merit pay (1981), the ERIC Clearinghouse on Educational Management noted that merit pay in American public education has been around since 1910. They also point out that the major difficulties cited in the development and administration of merit systems starts with the defining of "merit pay," the use of "money" in merit systems, the financing of such systems, and the acceptance of merit systems. Those persons arguing against merit systems point out that most every system that has been tried eventually has been discontinued. They also point out that it is not easy to objectively define good teaching.

The questions and problems associated with defining "what makes an effective or outstanding teacher" and then finding an evaluation tool to compare teachers are issues raised by White (1983) relative to merit pay systems for teachers (p. 10). She points to the negative aspects of merit being "employee stress, loss of significance for any reward except merit pay, competition among colleagues who are supposed to be working together, and serious morale problems." She goes on to state that one way to get away from peer competition is "to improve a system of group awards." It is interesting that White, who is an assistant editor in the AFT editorial department, still promotes the idea of "group award," or standard pay for all teachers whether they are good or bad. Her article, while purporting to look objectively at the merit pay issues, comes right back to the center stance taken by teacher unions relative to pay that rewards mediocre efforts and provides no incentive advantages to those faculty who may be making above average to superior efforts.

In a review of faculty awards, White (1983, p. 10) quoted Gary Sykes, former head of the teaching policies team at the National Institute of Education, as suggesting that the best way to reward outstanding teachers is to offer them expanded responsibilities and opportunities to develop professionally. He does not take into account, with this recommendation, that "expanded responsibilities" are not defined, possibly are not available in most small-to-medium-educational settings, and may pull the very best instructors out of the classrooms in which they are so desperately needed.

White does point out that those persons charged with doing the evaluations ". . . whether they are peers or supervisors—must be trained to do ratings based on objective criteria and to be as bias free as possible." This standard is, undoubtedly, more important than whether an evaluation and merit system exists for it is only through objective and bias free evaluations that the systems will take on credibility.

In a national study of 3,000 American schools designed to see how merit pay was being used or not used in these systems, Educational Research Service (ERS) found that only 4 percent of the schools had a merit pay plan. Some 6.4 percent of the schools indicated they had been into a merit system at one time but had abandoned continuation of the system. They also found that 4.7 percent were considering adoption of a merit plan (1979).

The ERIC research brief cited above pointed out that the merit pay issue may not be as bleak as those against merit pay would like to argue. They point out that nearly 90 percent of the schools in the ERS study "indicated no experience at all—good or bad—with merit pay."

In a related study, Hooker (1978, p. 481) points out that evaluation should be done by several persons who work cooperatively. He also states that evaluation guidelines should be "specific, multifaceted, and clearly articulated so that each evaluator assesses the same things." Hornbeck (1977) in his critical analysis of merit pay in the Pennsylvania educational system points out that it has not worked:

> Over the years the merit increments had, I think most would agree, deteriorated into a process in which a primary consideration was whether a particular faculty member had gotten one the year before or the year before that and whether that faculty member's turn to get one had come up again. (p. 453)

Deci (1976, pp. 61-72) points away from merit pay but offers an alternative as a result of his findings. He suggests a *positive feedback* system "that can, under certain circumstances, increase intrinsic motivation." He suggests a *praise* plan based on recognition may work better in motivating faculty through intrinsic satisfactions when persons "are complimented by the right kind of information." He sees this system as not being manipulated by the material rewards that merit pay systems provide.

A sample of a merit recognition plaque is presented as Exhibit 6.

While the rhetoric may dwell on such terms as *merit pay* or *master teacher,* Florio (1983, p. 16) says "the central issue is *teacher evaluation:* who decides, on what criteria, and in what way. Teacher assessment is at the crux of any program focused on teacher reward, advancement, and selection for additional duties."

Florio also challenges the educational researchers to be part of the politics of education that are emerging at the national level. The issues of merit pay and evaluation are now known and researchers can play a major contributing role. Their role could be a major factor in encouraging the 90 percent of the schools who have never attempted merit recognition systems to enter the arena.

Meyer (1975) feels a merit pay plan should involve many persons in its development stages, be pilot tested, and be implemented "slowly and carefully."

THE RESISTANCE TO MERIT

It is hard to determine where much of the resistance to merit pay and/or recognition systems evolves. In the Educational Research Service (ERS) national study (1979) it was found that nearly 90 percent of the schools surveyed had never experimented with any merit pay system. Much of the negative overtures appear to come from the large teacher unions which have consistently pushed for standardized pay scales for all faculty regardless of competency and productivity level. This tendency may be interpreted as an effort or striving to meet the "basic need" levels described by Maslow and Herzberg. It is easy to project that in most schools, which are strongly influenced by the unions' stance on standardized salary schedules, little to no attempt is made to experiment with any form of merit system.

The American Federation of Teachers and the National Education Association both reacted negatively and loudly to President Ronald Reagan's call for merit pay for outstanding teachers in the summer of 1983. Their response was that the basic pay for all teachers (basic needs) should be significantly upgraded. Such statements, while very true and necessary, quickly detract from meeting the needs of faculty to obtain some form of recognition for high-quality performances. This occurs while everyone waits for the across-the-board pay increases that are not likely to be granted in the immediate future.

SUMMARY

The merit pay, merit recognition, and evaluation issues are not likely to be forgotten quickly. National studies pointing to the severe condition of our schools came from several respectable sources during 1983. The President of the United States provided his own focus to the sorry state of education in the early 1980s by proposing "merit pay" for master teachers. The congressional study of the merit pay issue tripped over the *low faculty salaries* issue when proposing that some form of merit pay research and effort be forthcoming. Some significant legislation out of Washington is expected to focus on the Federal government's role in upgrading the state of education in the United States.

Faculty unions—while understandably cautious about seeing merit pay increases go to a few faculty when the total pay structure is so low in most states—must be involved in the coming merit recognition experimentation. There are human needs, as suggested by Maslow and Herzberg, that go wanting when standardized salary scales are used that pay the most competent and the least competent instructors the same dollar recognition for their efforts.

Some of the research on merit pay indicates that recognition and positive feedback may be much more effective in motivating those teachers who work for the intrinsic rewards of teaching than differential pay scales that compare instructors against each other.

"Excellence must result in reward," according to Sbaratta (1983, p. 27). He goes on to say that "without tangible and direct reward, the special talent and effort that produce excellence wither. Mediocrity and doing the minimum prevail, and the institution becomes anemic."

The merit pay or merit recognition issues presented in this chapter are highlighted as part of the major theme of this book: that quality instruction must be expected, that a strong administration evaluation system must be supported by boards of trustees and faculty, and that the results of that evaluation system should work "both ends of the curve" with the effect of improving the total instructional competence of the faculty (Andrews and Marzano, 1983-84, p. 36).

Definitely there is much room in educational institutions for improving the educational climate. The use of merit pay and/or a merit recognition system are ways to help promote the "positive skew" in performance that each secondary school and college should establish as one of its priority objectives.

Merit pay will receive a thorough test and review in the later part of the 1980s and the early 1990s. This author strongly supports the system as being administered by the administration and governing boards. Faculty concerns about "abuse" and "favoritism" are very real concerns. They must not be allowed to enter into a quality institution which prides itself on evaluating its staff for excellence. Excellence deserves to be rewarded. Merit pay is such a reward. Merit recognition may provide an alternative reward system which may be more acceptable to those schools and colleges that need an intermediate step.

Education can no longer afford to continue to neglect its very best talent. It is ridiculous to begin working to attract the brightest young people into a career in education and then later neglect their excellent contributions to the teaching field because administrators and governing boards are afraid to move away from a standardized pay scale via merit pay and merit recognition programs.

EXHIBIT 6

Illinois Valley COMMUNITY COLLEGE

1983
Merit
Recognition

MARJORIE HUNT

For

Outstanding Leadership In Secretarial

Program Development And Excellence

In Classroom Instruction

Division Chairman

President

Dean of Instruction

Chairman
Board of Trustees

10

"Poor teaching makes its own kind of difference; it stifles, deadens, and destroys whatever curiosity and enthusiasm students may bring to their studies. And its damage can be permanent."

—Wilkinson, 1982

Guiding the Evaluator: Negative Evaluation

IT WAS STATED EARLIER that excellence in the classroom *can not be assumed!* Faculty and academic support personnel in each secondary school, community college, or university have been hired over a long period of time by a number of administrators and board members. These persons in leadership roles may have been "turned over" several times over a five to twenty year period. There were times during the late 1950s and 1960s in which a teaching shortage existed. Recruitment of *highly qualified* faculty and academic support personnel was not always possible given the shortages that existed in some academic teaching disciplines over the years. There have been and will continue to be shortages of adequately qualified occupational and technical instructors in several teaching disciplines in the 1970s and into the late 1980s.

The American Association of Community and Junior colleges (AACJC) conducted a national study during 1982-1983 relative to the areas of critical shortages that existed for community and junior colleges. Computer science, electronics, and other high technology fields topped the list of immediate and existing shortages. The community and junior colleges and secondary vocational programs which are moving rapidly into new high technology fields of robotics, laser technology, micro-processors, etc. are finding these shortages even more critical. It may be sometime before these educational institutions will be financially ready to compete with business and industry to attract highly qualified personnel in the numbers needed. The non-competitive pay in education that exists nationally is not attractive to persons in business and industry and is likely to remain non-competitive for a considerable time.

In representative Carl D. Perkin's *Merit Pay Task Force Report* (1983), the one ingredient his task force points to as *"essential* to prevent imperiling the future economy and security of this country is a talented, dedicated teacher." His report vividly points out the problem of *low pay* of teachers in relationship to most other professionals (see Exhibit 7):

EXHIBIT 7

AVERAGE SALARY OF EMPLOYEES IN SELECTED WHITE COLLAR OCCUPATIONS IN PRIVATE ESTABLISHMENTS, MARCH, 1982

OCCUPATION	AVERAGE ANNUAL SALARY	OCCUPATIONAL CLASS AVERAGE ENTRY TO TOP LEVEL
Accountant	$26,306	$18,260 - 48,549
Attorney – salaried	43,249	25,162 - 76,202
Programmer/Analyst	24,809	17,535 - 35,430
Chemist	32,844	19,640 - 53,658
Engineer	34,745	23,622 - 52,494
Drafter	19,816	11,739 - 25,909
Computer Operator	16,231	11,896 - 23,267
Secretary	16,539	14,000 - 21,546
Typist	11,195	10,893 - 13,723
Teacher	18,945	12,966 - 23,437

Source: Calculations based on white collar salaries, March, 1982, U. S. Department of Labor, Bureau of Labor Statistics.

In another analysis of the current state of affairs in

education, Feistritzer (1983) points out the discrepancies that exist between education and other professions at both the entry level and 15 years later:

> Teacher salaries at entry—$12,769 for public elementary or secondary school beginning with a bachelor's degree—are almost $3,500 below starting pay for the next lowest professional, $16,200 for a college graduate in business administration, and considerably less than for the highest for the holder of a bachelor's degree, $20,364 in computer sciences. The worst news, however, is how the gap widens as the years go by—about $25,000 after 15 years for the teachers, $40,000 to $50,000 for, say, an accountant who started at $16,000. (p. 112)

Feistritzer credits this information to the National Education Association in its study of salaries in 1981-82.

THE QUALITY PROBLEM

The above statistics relative to critical personnel shortages and the non-competitive salaries paid to educators have been used to set the *backdrop* as to one of the major reasons governing boards and administrators *must not assume quality exists* in all classrooms within their institutions. These are realistic factors that have existed in the past and will continue to exist into the late-1980s and beyond.

One situation somewhat unique to community colleges is that they have gained a high visibility with their community service and outreach programs through the 1970s and early 1980s. They have presented businesses, industries, social agencies, chambers of commerce, and state and local governments with a responsiveness not formerly known in education. Specialized training programs, off-campus instruction, prison programs, re-training for the unemployed, and rapid movement into high technology programs have caused many new segments of the country to look to community colleges as *action agencies for change* and for improvements in the quality of life.

While becoming more things to more people, it becomes more important that the community colleges, secondary schools and universities not lose their thrust by tolerating less than *quality* instruction or academic support services.

Checking on quality should not be left to the non-professionals, such as students, who lack both the depth and experience to make judgments on quality or incompetence in the classroom or in the other services they receive. Peers have also been most ineffective in weeding out "one of their own" if quality is lacking. Most faculty do not want to be put into a judgmental role and that should be respected. Rood points that evaluations of teaching effectiveness and research capacity are not depriving faculty of their liberty rights:

> Evaluations of teaching effectiveness and research capacity, *even when negative* [emphasis added], have been construed as not depriving faculty members of liberty. (p. 137)

Administrative evaluators must be trained properly to know evaluational methodology, educational psychology, and how to properly assess classroom atmosphere and what is taking place during a lecture, lab, seminar, or in a counseling session. They need to know how to properly recognize quality performances and how to document them as was suggested in Chapter 6 under "Positive Evaluations." They also need to recognize a variety of *defects* and *deficiencies* in teaching or academic support personnel performances. This needs to be clearly documented so it can be conveyed to the person involved. Next, steps toward remediation of the problems needs to take place if the person evaluating wishes to have improvements made. As amazing as it will sound, administrative evaluators and governing boards will find some individuals stubbornly unwilling or academically unable to make the necessary suggested modifications in remediation of their problems.

The next few pages are devoted to providing some *examples of negative evaluation* in a number of the in-class teaching methodologies, student motivational techniques, classroom preparation, and proper subject and time management in which competence is expected, but not found, for some faculty who it "might be assumed" should be well qualified.

The same evaluation instrument as was used in Chapter 6 (positive evaluations) will be used to document defects and deficiencies of other faculty members. The reader may wish to return to Chapter 5 to review the sample evaluation form that was proposed and is used in the following illustrations.

EVALUATION QUESTIONS FROM THE EVALUATION FORM FOR FACULTY, ASSISTANTS TO INSTRUCTION, AND COUNSELORS

Question 1:

What evidence is there that the person *is* or *is not* prepared for this class, lab or counseling activity?

EXAMPLE 1: The "lecture" never really developed into any type of logical, progressive understanding of the principles that *must* be studied in this introductory principles class.

EXAMPLE 2: You must organize your classroom presentation in such a manner that your students are able to understand what you are trying to accomplish.

Question 2:

Is there evidence that there is appropriate homework, class participation, and other expectations of the students?

EXAMPLE 1: Twelve students were absent today. Note taking by students was not observed (cited in previous evaluations).

EXAMPLE 2: You need to communicate in writing what the requirements and specific expectations the students should know for successfully completing your courses.

Question 3:

Does the person use good teaching/counseling techniques and provide a good learning environment?

EXAMPLE 1: This class demands that students do homework assignments with each chapter. Yours are the only sections that students have the option of *not* doing the problems for the chapters.

EXAMPLE 2: Interact with as many of the students in the class as you can. You concentrated on only three again. This has been mentioned in two previous evaluations as a concern you need to work on.

Question 4:

Does the person demonstrate *adequate knowledge* of the subject, activity, or skill?

EXAMPLE 1: You have been observed discussing topics, at considerable length within your classes, which are not at all relevant to the teaching of your subject matter.

EXAMPLE 2: Concern has been presented by two of your evaluators relative to the need to spend time on the theory, definitions, and other material necessary to understanding the problems.

Question 5:

Is the discussion or activity germane to the *course syllabus?*

EXAMPLE 1: You covered two chapters that had been designated by the department to be left out. They will not be covered in the end-of-course departmental comprehensive exam.

Question 6:

What evidence is there that the *course syllabus* will be completed as required?

EXAMPLE 1: The instructor is four weeks behind his course outline. With only two hours of lecture remaining, once again it is impossible for him to complete the course syllabus in a semester.

Question 7:

Does the person evaluate student progress on a regular basis?

EXAMPLE 1: This instructor has not given one evaluation or exam to her students and the class is now in the tenth week of the semester. This is unexcusable!

EXAMPLE 2: We continue to receive complaints from her students relative to lack of testing and feedback. A check of both of her gradebooks from last year verifies this complaint as having substance.

Question 8:

Was sound use of testing and review techniques used where appropriate?

EXAMPLE 1: Over 50 minutes were devoted to a review of the last test. There was little explanation or clarification given as to why students scored so low on the test as a class.

EXAMPLE 2: Six chapters will be on next Friday's test. How can you properly test students over this material if 20 to 30 minutes is all that you will be able to devote to each of these six remaining complex chapters?

Question 9:

Are observed grading standards at a level to be expected for college?

EXAMPLE 1: This instructor was told she must discuss with the students her grading procedures and how the students' final grade will be determined. She did not do this in this initial class session.

EXAMPLE 2: Your grade distribution for the fall semester is in need of close review. A review of your grades show 63% received A's and 23 % received B's.

Question 10:

Does the person have meaningful interaction with the students?

EXAMPLE 1: You have not been observed asking any meaningful questions of your students during the class periods.

EXAMPLE 2: There is almost no interchange between the students and the instructor. She needs to try to involve the students and check their understanding of her lecture material.

EXAMPLE 3: The students were not questioned or brought into the lecture in any manner and, therefore, no real check was made on students' understanding of the material. The instructor commented that "you did this earlier in the semester" several times but she made no check to see if they had any recall.

Question 11:

Is the person able "to get materials across" and to answer student questions clearly?

EXAMPLE 1: Much work needs to be accomplished in working out *better explanations* in course materials and in response to student questions.

EXAMPLE 2: Your students scored significantly lower on the departmental exam than any other instructors, full-time or part-time, in the basic courses during both of the previous semesters.

OTHER PROFESSIONAL RESPONSIBILITIES

Question 1:

Does the person maintain attendance records as required by the college and state?

EXAMPLE 1: You have not been observed taking roll in any of the class sessions we have evaluated this semester. You are aware that student attendance must be recorded for each session.

EXAMPLE 2: No attendance was taken today. The student handbook, faculty handbook, and state regulation all require attendance to be taken. Over one-third of her class was absent.

Question 2:

Does the person attend and participate in faculty meetings, division meetings, and college committees?

EXAMPLE 1: You have missed three department meetings this semester. Please stop by my office to review the situation.

EXAMPLE 2: This instructor has not adequately carried out her responsibilities on the curriculum committee this year. She missed 3 of the 9 meetings and twice failed to prepare reports as assigned.

Question 3:

Does the person keep current on the latest developments in his or her field of study?

EXAMPLE 1: You have not applied for a state or national professional meeting in the past five years. You are being asked to take the initiative to attend an appropriate state meeting this semester. Please work with your division chairperson.

Question 4:

Does the person exhibit a positive working relationship with colleagues and the administration?

EXAMPLE 1: On three separate occasions your supervisors have requested that you come to their offices to discuss with them your written classroom evaluations. You have ignored all three requests. This is a direct act of insubordination.

EXAMPLE 2: When you were told that you would not be assigned the summer school class because of your neglect of my recommendations for your classroom improvement, you became angry and began a tirade of abusive and profane language toward me. This letter is to inform you that such an outburst of behavior will not be tolerated in the future.

SUMMARY

Evaluating tenured faculty and academic support personnel negatively is a tremendously difficult but necessary challenge for administrators. There should be no pride for an administrator who goes home at night knowing his or her *inaction* in the evaluation of staff has allowed defects and deficiencies in their work to continue. An administrator must consider the 120-175 students each semester who are exposed to incompetent faculty performance the school may be condoning without attempting to correct and remediate such behavior, or to take the steps necessary to move toward a dismissal.

Bevan suggests that "it's important to remember that both positive and negative recognition is more effective for learning than no recognition at all" (1980, p. 15). Incompetent performances in a secondary school or a community college are not sheltered by the same dynamics that exist in four-year colleges and universities. High school and community college students do not retreat to a dormitory or to private apartments when the day ends. They return to their homes, families, and high schools which become ready audiences to learn about the "quality" or "lack of it" in their classrooms at school. An incompetent secondary school or community college instructor can not find outlets such as research and publishing activities to hide their poor classroom performances behind. These simply are not parts of the job requirements of either secondary school or community college faculty members.

Rood (1977) pointed out that termination of faculty members today may well mean "removal from a profession, not just a position. Not only are openings few," he said, "but budget reductions tend to restrict appointments to minimum salaries." He goes on to say, "that under these conditions the decision to try to stay, protest, and if necessary fight a dismissal, rather than leave, becomes attractive" (p. 23).

While shortages of faculty in certain fields exist and low pay provides tremendous competition in attracting the highest quality and qualified personnel, these circumstances do not provide adequate rationale for the acceptance of and continuation of *incompetent* performances by tenured faculty or academic support personnel.

11

Guiding the Board: Some Practical Discussion on Preparing A Notice To Remedy

WHILE IT IS ASSUMED that most faculty and academic support personnel on tenure status are supporting their institution and students with average to superior performances, it is naive to think that all of them are at all times. An effective administrative evaluation system can and should document areas of concern and problems that will be referred to as *defects* and *deficiencies* throughout this chapter.

There are numerous defects and deficiencies which may be documented. They can be as numerous as the "straw-person" characteristics of an effective instructor (or academic support person) outlined in Chapter 1. The sample evaluation form from Chapter 5 is the type of document upon which these defects and deficiencies should be recorded. Post-evaluation conferences between the faculty member and the administrative evaluator(s) should be used to discuss the defects and/or deficiencies in the written evaluation form. The final step in this initial evaluation discussion should be for the faculty member to be given written suggestions on how to remedy the problem(s) *or* to have the faculty member make suggestions on how he or she will address the defects and/or deficiencies. It is during this conference that any misperceptions the evaluator(s) may have made in their evaluation can be clarified. Legitimate misperceptions should be rewritten into the evaluation form as a correction prior to the signing of the evaluation form and placing it into the faculty member's personnel folder. If subsequent evaluations continue to document the same defects and deficiencies in one's teaching or other job responsibilities, and adequate adjustments are not made, the administrators should consider their next remediation steps. What those steps should be will depend upon the requirements of the tenure laws of the state in which the secondary school or college resides.

THE NOTICE TO REMEDY

The tenure law that went into existence in Illinois for community colleges in 1980 did not make specific reference to the need for a notice to remedy from the boards of trustees prior to a tenured faculty or academic support person's dismissal. The common school law in Illinois does, however, require a notice to remedy. The significance of this becomes apparent when one analyzes how similar the community college tenure law is to the common school tenure law in all other aspects of its provisions. Rapp and Ortbal (1980), in their review of the impact of the Illinois tenure law, point out that most reversals in the courts of fired tenure faculty in the common schools is due to the *failure of boards to give notice to remedy.* They point out that "if the reasons for dismissal are considered *remediable,* a board must give the teacher reasonable warning in writing stating the causes of dismissal which, if not removed, may result in charges and dismissal (p. 39).

There are other considerations on whether a notice to remedy should be given or if an administrative evaluation should be taken directly to the governing board as a recommendation for dismissal. There is a "shock effect" to be dealt with. Staff dismissal may be new to a secondary school or college which has not previously evaluated their tenured faculty. Boards may see a notice to remedy as a intermediate and *fair* warning that they will not tolerate further evidence of the defects and deficiencies cited. It also gives boards a guide for evaluating possible future dismissal action. The board will be able to see if their notice to remedy items were followed or ignored. Faculty unions and other faculty organizations which may be suspicious of newly introduced administrative evaluation procedures will also view the notice to remedy less shocking and fairer than a quick dismissal action. Faculty members who are involved in such a notice will find that the matter is indeed serious but that they are given further opportunity to remediate their defects and deficiencies.

The notice to remedy gives the administrators involved some clear direction and support from the governing board. They will know their work in a tough evaluation situation has received close board scrutiny and is being endorsed by the board as it votes to issue the faculty member an *official notice to remedy*.

STEPS TOWARD A NOTICE TO REMEDY

There are several steps that need to be taken prior to going to the governing board with a recommendation to issue a notice to remedy. The first step is to clearly identify the areas of concern during the formal administrative evaluation process. The following questions and responses are examples of defects and deficiencies that can be documented by administrative personnel during classroom evaluations over a period of time:

Example 1 (Classroom evaluation notes)

Q. Does the person use good teaching techniques and provide a good learning environment?

COMMENTS BY EVALUATOR:

A. The instructor appears to demand no effort on the part of his students:
   (1) No attendance is required (19 out of 27 students were absent for this class today);
   (2) Little to no homework in this class is required by the instructor;
   (3) No class participation is used.

The following example is a documented case of insubordination by the same instructor to his division chairperson:

Example 2 (Administrative reprimand for insubordination and neglect of professional activities outside of the classroom)

Memorandum to Instructor:

> This memorandum should serve as an official administrative reprimand.
>
> (1) Lack of updating course syllabi for your courses after several warnings;
> (2) Refusal to attend advisory committee and faculty meetings when directed to do so by your division chairperson.
>
> This insubordination will no longer be tolerated. Any further evidence of insubordination will be cause for a Board of Trustee review of your situation.

It is important that evaluation continues through the various stages outlined—in extreme cases such as those suggested above—in the above examples. The instructor has been given specific defects and deficiencies to correct.

Once an instructor has reached an intense level of evaluation, it is important that all available sources of information about the instructor be analyzed in order to further clarify the problems and suggest possible solutions.

Example 3 (Follow-up memorandum to a review of the faculty member's grading and attendance book system.)

TO: Instructor

RE: A Review of Your Grading/Attendance Records

Your attendance records for the fall semester have been thoroughly reviewed. We have found a pattern of excessive documented absences in each of your four classes that were reviewed. This documented pattern correlates very closely with the written evaluations of your administrative supervisors this past semester.

At an earlier date you told us that you require students to be in attendance as stated in the college's attendance policy. We are submitting the attached summary document which strongly indicates the opposite is true.

A SUMMARY OF ATTENDANCE POLICY ABUSE FOUND IN THE CLASSES OF
_____, INSTRUCTOR
Fall Semester

INDIVIDUAL EXCESSIVE ABSENCES

Number of Absences	Students' Last Name	Final Grade
24	(Jones)	A
31	(Vedock)	B
21	(Barr)	C
21	(Branstetter)	B
24	(Smith)	C-
27	(Hamilton)	B
30	(Donahue)	B-

Example 4 (Classroom evaluation of the first class of the new semester.)

Evaluation Question: Is there evidence of good instructor student relationships?

Evaluator Comments: There was no evidence of this. There was not one word exchanged between the instructor and the students. Students were talking with each other, laughing, and were otherwise not attentive.

Example 5 (Follow-up memorandum to meeting of the division chairperson with the instructor relative to the above classroom evaluation.)

TO: Instructor

RE: Our Review of Classroom Evaluation

It was apparent that you were unwilling to accept any of my observations or suggestions for improvement relative to the recent classroom evaluation I made:

(A) When I pointed out that the overview of your course lasted one hour and forty-five minutes which was a waste of valuable lecture time, your response was "but that's the way I have always done it."

(B) When I pointed out there appeared to be little or no planning for your lecture, again you stated "but that's the way I have always done it."

You continue to disregard any of the efforts that we have put forth to assist you.

DECISION TIME FOR A NOTICE TO REMEDY

It is obvious that the instructor portrayed in the above examples has been evaluated as having several defects and deficiencies. Even more disturbing is the fact that he does not appear to be making the adaptations requested of him. Subsequent evaluations by his division chairperson and dean of instruction provide further evidence of the same defects and deficiencies that were outlined over the previous five-month period. It becomes obvious now that the months of effort to assist this instructor in adapting his classroom teaching to meet student needs and expectations and other job responsibilities have not paid off.

The administrators' next step is to notify the college president they are ready to recommend that a formal notice to remedy be taken to the board of trustees to consider for action. The administrators will prepare a written summary of the defects and deficiencies as outlined in "Exhibit 8". In addition to "Exhibit 8" the board members will be given a booklet containing copies of all the classroom evaluations and other documents that have been put in written form. Any insubordination notices also will be included. This documentation will give the governing board the assurances they need to know that quality administrative efforts have been made prior to bringing the instructor's defects and deficiencies to their attention. They also will be able to *track* the administrator's future efforts to remediate these defects and deficiencies.

EXHIBIT 8

LIST OF DEFECTS AND DEFICIENCIES IN THE TEACHING AND OVERALL JOB PERFORMANCE OF _____

1. *Insubordination.*

   There has been a consistent pattern of insubordination involving you and your immediate supervisor in recent months.

2. *Failure to work with other faculty members and your supervisor* in bringing about *curriculum improvements and program changes* as required in your teaching area.

3. *Lack of Communicating "Student Expectations"* to Your Students.

   Students in your courses need to be informed by you as to what expectations and requirements they should have for successfully completing the courses.

4. *Failure to make your examinations demanding and challenging* to your students in a manner appropriate for this level of work.

   You have been reprimanded by your supervisors for failing to develop appropriate examinations with the proper degree of difficulty and challenge for college-level students.

5. *Failure to demonstrate a positive and enthusiastic attitude* in your teaching assignments.

   You should work to develop a more pleasant disposition and a genuine enthusiastic attitude when teaching your classes. You should develop a relaxed, yet professional demeanor in the classroom to allow for better student-instructor interaction.

6. *Conclusion.*

   These defects and deficiencies have been observed in your classroom presentations and in job related activities. It is incumbent that you seriously evaluate these concerns and make the necessary adjustments and changes in your attitude and manner of teaching to correct and remediate these problems. You should meet with your administrative supervisors as soon as possible to outline your course of action for correcting these defects and deficiencies.

Discussion concerning the defects and deficiencies of the instructor should usually be accomplished in an *executive session* of the governing board. If the action the board decides to take is in support of the administrative recommendation, the action may have to take place in open public session in those states that have a "sunshine" law for board actions. It may be possible that a waiver to public notice can be pre-arranged with the instructor prior to the board of trustees executive meetings. Exhibit 8 is an example of such a waiver form. In this case the faculty member is notified that the board has reviewed the recommendation of the administration. The college president then may be directed to notify the instructor that the board is supportive of the notice to remedy, and direct the faculty member to meet in the immediate future with his administrative supervisors to work out a plan to remediate the items in "Exhibit 8" which itemizes the defects and deficiencies. The waiver form may have much more appeal to faculty unions and other faculty groups who fear that public notice will do additional damage to the opportunities the faculty member will have to remediate his problems in the months ahead.

EXHIBIT 9

WAIVER OF PUBLIC WARNING

NOTICE TO REMEDY DIRECTLY
FROM THE BOARD OF TRUSTEES
Illinois Valley Community College

I acknowledge receipt of the attached notice of alleged defects in my teaching, performance or job conduct and I understand that I have the option to receive the notice directly from the Board of Trustees.

I do hereby elect to receive the attached notice under the signature of the President and I do hereby freely waive any right I may have to receive the warning notice directly from the Board. I do also hereby waive any right to object to the sufficiency of the warning notice based upon the fact that it has been given to me by the President of the College. I accept the attached warning notice in satisfaction of any procedural due process rights I may have to a warning that there are alleged defects in my performance or conduct which may result in charges for my dismissal.

DATED _____.

_____
Instructor

WITNESSES:

_____

_____

Subscribed and sworn to before me

This _____ day of _____ 1985

_____
Notary

(seal)

TRANSMITTING THE NOTICE TO REMEDY TO THE INSTRUCTOR

The notice to remedy, once approved by formal action of the governing board must be transmitted to the instructor. In most cases a letter from the chairperson of the board is in order. In those cases where a "Waiver of Public Warning" has been worked out in executive session, the board of trustees may direct the president to notify the instructor of their grave concerns and expectations to see remediation take place on the part of the instructor. The following is a copy of a sample letter that may be sent directly by the board chairperson within a day or more following the board action:

EXHIBIT 10

BOARD CHAIRPERSON'S LETTER

April 12, 1985

_____

_____

_____

Dear _____:

   We regret to inform you that your teaching and overall job performance are of such a concern that we are issuing you the attached resolution and list of defects and deficiencies that need to be overcome. We feel this is of a serious enough nature to issue you a formal warning and to let you know that if your performance does not improve, you will be dismissed as provided for in the State Faculty Tenure Law.

   The attached resolution was passed by the _____ Board of Trustees at its regularly scheduled meeting on Tuesday, June 14, 1984. The defects and deficiencies listed and described in the Board's resolution are not new and have been brought to your attention in communications by your administrative supervisors.

   Your administrative supervisors discussed the need for you to make some attempt to enrich your classroom presentations, use more audio visuals, consider professional upgrading, and some outreach efforts similar to what they had been suggesting to other faculty at that time. They again pointed out the need to upgrade and update your professional schooling during this past year when the topic of "faculty competencies" was a major issue. In trying to determine if some improvements would be necessary within your classes to aid you in attracting and holding students, administrators have found some very severe defects and deficiencies in your teaching and other job responsibilities. It is the severe nature of these defects and deficiencies that makes Board action necessary at this time.

   You should thoroughly read and regard all of the defects and deficiencies as equally significant and you are advised that you are to eliminate all of these deficiencies. The elimination of some of the defects and deficiencies will not be sufficient. We hope the listing of these defects and deficiencies will be self-evident and your behavior will be appropriately changed to eliminate them.

You are being directed to meet with your administrative supervisors as soon as it is practical after your receipt of this letter to discuss the specific measures which you will be taking to commence remediation of the cited defects and deficiencies. During the remainder of the spring semester, your supervisors will work with you and continue to evaluate you in an attempt to improve your teaching and other job responsibilities.

Most sincerely,

_____
Chairperson, Board of Trustees

_____
Secretary, Board of Trustees

Along with the letter from the board chairperson, a formal resolution entitled "Authorizing a List of Defects and Deficiencies in the Teaching and Other Job Performance of _____" will be sent to the instructor in question. The following is a sample of such a board resolution (Exhibit 11):

EXHIBIT 11
GOVERNING BOARD RESOLUTION
RESOLUTION RE: _____
AUTHORIZING LIST OF DEFECTS AND DEFICIENCIES IN TEACHING AND OTHER JOB PERFORMANCE OF _____

WHEREAS, this Board of Trustees has received from the administration regarding the teaching and overall job performance of _____ as a full-time tenured faculty member of this college district; and,

WHEREAS, this Board hereby finds and determines that such reports state causes, charges, reasons, and defects in the teaching and overall job performance of _____ which, if not removed, are causes, charges, and reasons warranting discharge and dismissal of _____ as a faculty member of this college district; and,

WHEREAS, this Board herewith finds and determines that the teaching and overall job performance of _____, to date, in this district has been of an unsatisfactory nature;

Now, THEREFORE, Be It Resolved by the Board of Trustees of this Community College District as follows:

SECTION 1: That the Chairman and Secretary of this Board of Trustees are hereby authorized and directed to sign and serve or cause to be served on behalf of the Board of Trustees upon _____ a List of Defects and Deficiencies in the Teaching and Overall Job Performance of _____ substantially in the form of Exhibit 1 attached hereto and made a part hereof, which List of Defects and Deficiencies enumerates causes, charges, reasons, and defects which this Board determines, if not remedied, may result in the discharge and dismissal of _____ as a faculty member in this college district.

SECTION 2: This resolution shall be in full force and effect forthwith upon its adoption.

Adopted this _____ day of _____, 19____, by the following roll call vote:

AYES: 7
NAYS: 0
ABSENT: 0

_____
Chairperson, Board of Trustees

_____
Secretary, Board of Trustees

SUMMARY

Evaluations of faculty and academic support personnel that are of a negative nature will occur for a small percentage of any institution's faculty. When administrative evaluations spot and document some defects and deficiencies in teaching and other aspects of the total job, every effort should be taken to assist the instructor or academic support person to become aware of such evaluation. Suggestions by both the evaluator and faculty member will need to be made in an effort to remediate the defects and deficiencies.

Several examples of subsequent evaluations, meetings, and follow-up evaluations were presented in this chapter.

There will be situations that call for a notice to remedy when behavior does not change and the defects and deficiencies continue to exist. The notice to remedy should be made to the college president who should evaluate it prior to taking it to the governing board for possible action. The president's decision will, undoubtedly, be tempered and decided with legal counsel at this point. The formal notice to remedy needs to be made by the college's board of trustees and properly transmitted to the faculty member involved.

A notice to remedy may not be always called for in tenure laws in various states. It is, however, a safeguard prior to going into a judicial system which may be tempered to consider many defects and deficiencies as being remediable. It is important that legal counsel for the institution assist in determining if the governing board should consider the notice to remedy option.

12

"School boards should deal with personnel in good faith, follow statutory procedures for dismissal, provide due-process procedures, and use the services of an attorney in securing advice."

—Garber, 1956a

Guiding the Board: Preparing for Just Cause Dismissals of Faculty

THE BOARD OF TRUSTEES' issuance of a *notice to remedy* to a faculty member is a clear signal that administrative evaluation of the instructor will continue. The faculty member will have been directed by the board chairperson to discuss the particulars in the notice to remedy with his or her immediate supervisors.

The next several months will become crucial for the faculty member. Closer administrative evaluation will be expected by both the board of trustees and the faculty member involved.

The administrative evaluators will need to use the items listed in the notice to remedy as a guide to record any progress or lack of progress by the faculty person. The following is developed as a progress report following a meeting with an instructor after ten in-class evaluations over a semester following a notice to remedy on January 18, 1983:

> **RE: Follow-Up of Meeting on May 1**
> **to Discuss Your In-Class Evaluation**
> **Since the January Notice to Remedy**

NOTICE TO REMEDY, ITEM 1: You were told to follow your course syllabus and to quit disregarding topics which are necessary to complete your beginning course syllabi.

PROGRESS: You have once again shown a flagrant disregard for completing the syllabi outlined for this course, Mr. Brown. Five major topical areas were once again left out. The warning you were given six weeks ago at mid-semester was not followed.

NOTICE TO REMEDY, ITEM 2: Poor use of lecture time in your courses.

PROGRESS: Our classroom visitations have found you continuing to lecture without any order. Your lecture rambles, you go from topic-to-topic without any apparent use of notes or sequence. This has been documented in all seven administrative classroom evaluations this semester.

NOTICE TO REMEDY, ITEM 3: Testing procedures and use of evaluation are very poor.

PROGRESS: You failed to return the last exam in your 2:00 p.m. class. Students asked for it and you were not ready to return it, discuss it, or give out grades. The lecture time to do this is gone now with final exams week here.

NOTICE TO REMEDY, ITEM 4: You were told to attend professional meetings in your field. You had not taken a course or attended a professional meeting in three (3) years.

PROGRESS: (1) you have disregarded this directive and attended no professional meetings all semester.

The most serious defect in your work is your failure to complete the major material in the course syllabi. This course is articulated to four-year colleges and universities. It is important for you to complete the course for students who plan to transfer.

THE ATTORNEY'S OPINION

Once a notice to remedy has been issued to a faculty member, it is important that the college administrators keep their legal advisor updated on any progress or lack of progress in the remediation of the notice to remedy. It is important that the attorney feel comfortable with the documentation when the faculty member is failing to make sufficient progress and before a movement to dismiss a tenured faculty member occurs.

In determining what the courts have permitted to count

as contributing to incompetence, Strike and Bull (1981)
have summarized the following:

> On the basis of such remarks, Rosenberger and Plimpton
> (1975) conclude that "There seems to have been no legal
> need to define competence" (p. 470), and that "conventional
> wisdom and common sense, rather than precise standards,
> have been used in judging incompetence claims" (p. 486).

Legal counsel may suggest that evaluation should continue. It may take at least another semester to properly
evaluate the progress (or lack of it) on the faculty member's
part.

A ROLE FOR FACULTY UNIONS

Faculty unions have developed as a significant force
in colleges and secondary schools in several states over the
last decade. Further growth is expected throughout the
1980s and beyond.

During the summer of 1983, Albert Shanker, President
of the American Federation of Teachers (A.F.T.), in an
interview by Gallagher in the *Chicago Tribune* (1983),
indicated that his union may need to change its stance on
faculty evaluation. He indicated that they had always considered evaluation and dismissal of incompetent faculty
members strictly the problem of the administrators. He
said in the same interview that the union may now need to
change its approach and accept some of the responsibility
for getting incompetent faculty members out of its ranks.

Administrators should consider how the faculty union
leadership can play a role in negative faculty evaluation
situations. There is much to be gained by the union representatives' involvement in evaluation sessions for faculty
members who are in trouble. First, the union representatives
get the facts firsthand on what has been evaluated negatively.
Secondly, they will see how the faculty member reacts to the
evaluation and suggestions for improvement. Some of the
faculty they observe will deny any defects or deficiencies
in their teaching or other job responsibilities and will reject
any administrative suggestions for improvement. They may
refuse to make suggestions themselves. Other faculty

members will admit to the observed defects and deficiencies and will want immediate suggestions and assistance to remedy shortcomings as quickly as possible.

Much of the emotion that builds up as a faculty member's case moves toward a board of trustee notice to remedy and/or a dismissal will be dissipated if the union observes the process step-by-step and is somewhat involved. This author believes that faculty union opposition to administrative evaluation systems will change as the union leadership at the national and state levels begin to assert themselves as responsible partners in improving the quality of education and as being opposed to protecting incompetent instructors in their ranks. Such statements as those of Albert Shanken (A.F.T.) will go a long way in providing a unified board of trustees, administration, and faculty union (leadership) team approach to eliminating incompetence in education. The withdrawal of union financial support to those faculty members who are dismissed due to their incompetence and/or refusal to remedy their defects and deficiencies is a necessary step in a system such as is being proposed.

Surely, the cause of quality education in American and Canadian secondary schools and community colleges is not aided when faculty organizations support the cause of known incompetent instructors in the courts and flight boards of trustees and administrators in their efforts to improve a school or college's quality and image. Much of the basis for higher salaries and community respect for educators is lost in such transactions.

DECISION TIME ON DISMISSAL

The sample case presented earlier appears to be reaching a peak, because after much close evaluation following the board of trustees' notice to remedy, very little to no progress has occurred.

Proving incompetence is not an issue that can be taken lightly by a board of trustees or an administrative staff. Strike and Bull (1981) point out that judicial opinion on what is incompetence and how it may be proven is not unanimous. Courts do not take this issue lightly. They state:

First, courts are likely to rely on the professional judgment of administrators in the substantive aspects of evaluation. In one recent case, a federal appeals court remarked
as follows: "It is possible that the discretion of a Board may,
at times, to those more generously endowed, seem to have
been exercised with with a lack of wisdom. But the Board's
decisions in the exercise of its discretion are not vulnerable
to our correction merely if they are 'wrong,' sustainable only
if they are 'right'. . . . Such matters as the competence of
teachers, and the standards of its measurement are not,
without more, matters of constitutional dimensions. They are
peculiarly appropriate to state and local administration"
(Scheelhaase v. Woodbury Central Community School District).

Second, however, judicial review of dismissal decisions
is likely to be more restrictive when dealing with the procedural aspects of dismissal. Courts require that legislated
or contractual procedures for evaluation or due process be
rigorously followed. Moreover, they insist that evidence be
produced that clearly demonstrates a significant failure on
the part of the teacher. They may also insist, where the defects
are remediable, that opportunity for improvement be given
(Yesinowski v. Board of Education). And granting tenure to
a teacher creates presumption in favor of the competence
of the teacher, which must be disproven.

Third, despite the lack of an authoritative legal definition
and despite jurisdictional variations in interpretation, a
general and widely accepted core of meaning for teaching
incompetence can be discerned in the case law. Incompetence
may stem from deficiencies in the teacher's own knowledge
of the subject matter to be taught, from inability to impart
that knowledge, or from inability to maintain appropriate
classroom discipline (4 ALR 3rd 1094). Moreover, incompetence is to be reflected in a pervasive pattern of teacher
behavior that has proven to be irremediable (22 Proof of
Facts 64-69). (pp. 324-325)

It is important that the college's attorney has reviewed
in total all of the documents and facts in the case. The
college president must agree and may need to meet in an
executive session with his or her board of trustees. Such a
meeting will bring the board up-to-date on the administrative efforts to assist the faculty member to remediate the
defects and deficiencies which had been cited in their notice
to remedy. If the board agrees with their president's and
attorney's recommendation, they may ask the attorney to
prepare them to move toward a dismissal of the faculty
member.

LEGAL REQUIREMENTS

It now becomes extremely important that a well documented case leading to a board of trustees decision to fire a faculty or academic support person not be lost because of procedural mismanagement. If a state has a legislated tenure law spelling out the "Dismissal of Tenured Faculty Member for Cause," it should be followed step-by-step. The Illinois Community College Tenure Law has such a provision and has the following requirements in it:

1. The board must first approve a motion by a majority vote of all its members.

2. The specific charges for dismissal shall be confidential but shall be issued to the faculty member upon request.

3. The board decision shall be final unless the tenured faculty member within ten days requests in writing to the board that a hearing be scheduled.

4. Such notice shall contain a bill of particulars.

5. All testimony at the hearing shall be taken under oath administered by the hearing officer.

6. The hearing officer shall, with reasonable dispatch, make a decision as to whether or not the tenured member shall be dismissed and shall give a copy of the decision to both the tenured faculty member and the board.

7. The decision of the hearing officer shall be final and binding.

There are other procedural statements in the law as to how to select a hearing officer, subpoenaing witnesses, costs, etc. Strike and Bull (1981) summarize five indirect implications relative to teacher evaluation procedures which may lead to the termination of teachers:

> First, evaluations should be undertaken on a regular basis. Second, permanent records of the results of evaluations should be maintained. Third, teachers should be informed of the evaluation results, including access to their personnel file. These policies allow evaluations to be used

to establish the irremediable nature of the defects upon which a judgment of incompetence is based. Fourth, teachers should be given an opportunity to enter explanations and clarifications of or objections to particular evaluation findings into their personnel record at the time at which those findings are filed. Fifth, the evaluation records should be kept confidential. (p. 339)

REQUEST FOR HEARING RELATIVE TO DISMISSAL

The faculty member being dismissed may file for a hearing relative to the dismissal. He or she may also request and receive the list of reasons for the dismissal as approved by the board of trustees.

The following sample letter could be used to transmit the list of reasons and provide the board with a record of such transmittal. The list of reasons in Mr. Brown's case are also attached.

June 16, 1983

Dear Mr. Brown:

Pursuant to your request and in accord with the Illinois Community College Tenure Act, you are hereby provided a list of the charges for your dismissal and a bill of particulars covering these charges.

Sincerely,

President

Enclosure

cc: Members of the Board of Trustees
Community College District No. 711

NOTICE OF CHARGES
AND
BILL OF PARTICULARS

Pursuant to the Illinois Community College Tenure Act, you are hereby provided with a list of the charges for your dismissal and a Bill of Particulars covering those charges.

I. YOU HAVE DISREGARDED THE OFFICIAL COLLEGE COURSE
SYLLABUS IN TEACHING YOUR COURSES.

The following are *other reasons* that Mr. Brown would receive. Each one would have a number of examples of the continuing defects and deficiencies as were observed and documented.

II. YOU CONTINUE TO NOT PROPERLY PREPARE FOR AND
MANAGE YOUR LECTURE TIME.

III. FAILURE TO IMPROVE EVALUATION AND TESTING.

IV. FAILURE TO ENGAGE IN ANY ATTEMPTS TO UPGRADE YOUR
COMPETENCE AS A PROFESSIONAL.

V. YOU HAVE BEEN PERSISTENTLY NEGLIGENT IN CARRYING
OUT YOUR DUTIES AS A FACULTY MEMBER.

THE SEVEN TESTS FOR "JUST CAUSE"

The arbitration hearing may take from several weeks to several months before it is finally scheduled to the satisfaction of both parties. There are a number of "tests" that have become guides for arbitrators in their quest for determining whether an employer fired an employee for "just cause." The following is such a list developed by Carroll R. Daughterty (Baer, 1974, p. 88):

1. Did the employer give to the employee forewarning or foreknowledge of the possible or probable disciplinary consequences of the employee's conduct?

2. Was the employer's rule or managerial order reasonably related to the orderly, efficient, and safe operation of the employer's business?

3. Did the employer, before administering discipline to an employee, make an effort to discover whether the employee did in fact violate or disobey a rule or order of management?

4. Was the employer's investigation conducted fairly and objectively?

5. At the investigation did the "judge" obtain substantial evidence or proof that the employee was guilty as charged?

6. Has the employer applied its rules, orders, and penalties even-handedly and without discrimination to all employees?

7. Was the degree of discipline administered by the employer in a particular case reasonably related to (a) the seriousness of the employee's proven offense and (b) the record of the employee in his service with the employer?

If it is found that an employer has neglected one or more of the above tests before making the decision on the dismissal of the employee, it is very likely the arbitrator will find the employer had some element of arbitrary, capricious, unreasonable, or discriminatory action in its decision. In those cases the arbitrator is likely to return a decision that reverses the employer's decision to terminate the employee.

The scheduling of the hearing is another step in the legal process and must be responded to by the board of trustees if a dismissed employee so requests a hearing. Rood (1977) has described the benefits of a hearing for the administration (and board of trustees) as follows:

> From the administrative point of view, the hearing may provide both the administration and the board with an additional source of information and an opportunity to review the initial decision. Where facts are not as originally perceived, the hearing allows the institution to make appropriate adjustments and perhaps avoid court action. In any case, providing a hearing, whether or not required, avoids the appearance that the administration has something to hide. Rather than a threat to administrative authority (as some administrators view hearings), hearings ought to be regarded as an additional means of executing administrative responsibility. (p. 143)

SUMMARY

The decision to terminate a tenured faculty member can be a long and laborious process for a college administration and board of trustees. Such a decision must be handled objectively, reasonably, non-discriminatorily, and *must not be done in an arbitrary manner.*

The author has previously recommended the use of a notice to remedy as an intermediate step prior to any possible dismissal action by a board of trustees. Administrative evaluation following the notice to remedy will be done around a specific list of defects and deficiencies to evaluate.

The administrative evaluators will need to continue in-class and other job responsibility evaluations and to document their findings. They need to continue to meet with the faculty member to review their findings of improvements or lack of significant remediation steps by the instructor. Such evaluation may be necessary for several months or longer. The instructor must continually be made aware that *all* items in the notice to remedy must be remediated and not just the ones he or she chooses to remedy.

The *decision* to move for a termination of a tenured faculty or academic support person needs close review by the board's legal counsel. The administrators, president, and legal counsel must feel ready and comfortable with the decision to recommend dismissal to the board of trustees. All persons involved, including individual board members, will feel the pressure involved in such a decision. The author has pointed out a faculty union role in the remediation process from the notice to remedy through the point of decision on dismissal. Such a role by the faculty union can be supplemental to the administration's efforts to assist in the remediation of the faculty member's defects and deficiencies.

Administrators and boards must use the same type of objective *tests* that an arbitrator uses in order to see if they have been fair in their decision and the time allotted for remediation.

The firing of a long-term tenured faculty or academic support person can be a very traumatic decision. There is much emotion to be expected when such a decision is made. It can, however, provide a cleansing effect for a college or public school faculty, administration, and governing board who are all aware that they have some *deadwood* and incompetent instructors in their ranks. The spin-off effects of a healthy anxiety among some other faculty and academic support personnel may well lead to improved performances in their jobs. This will then result in improved instruction and services for hundreds or thousands of students in secondary schools or colleges that *will not tolerate* incompetent faculty performances for their students!

13

Conclusion

THE MOVEMENT TOWARD 'EXCELLENCE' in
secondary schools, community colleges, and four year
colleges and universities in the mid-1980s is presenting
some very shallow solutions in trying to respond to the
critical national studies on the American educational system!

Raising the standards for students, while appearing to
be an admirable move on the part of many state legislatures
and educational districts, is only providing diversion away
from the more critical issue of faculty competency and
qualifications which remain in a static state. In fact, the
retrenchments of younger faculty (more competent than
many of those who have been retained due to strict seniority
systems) is actually a movement in the opposite direction.
Curriculum changes, movement back to the basics, and
better equipment are only surface movements toward the
quality or 'excellence' issue that the American society has
demanded in the mid-to late-1980s.

The key ingredient to the successful movement into
'excellence' in education is that of quality in the faculty
of any educational institution. This author has presented
a thorough discussion on why quality in the classroom cannot
be assumed. Faculty must be screened thoroughly when
being hired, be evaluated extremely carefully prior to any
decision on tenure, and receive continual evaluation throughout their tenured teaching careers.

Excellence in education will not be achieved through

student-, peer-, or self-evaluation systems. Competent administrators, properly supported by governing boards with sound board policies on evaluation can and must make the difference. If student-, peer-, and self-evaluation systems worked, we would not have reached such a low level of respect as documented in the recent national studies. Why does the literature not show any faculty firings based upon these three systems? The reasons appear to evolve clearly from the research presented earlier in the book. They are systems that have no accountability in law (only the governing boards can hire or fire), do not have responsibility for action by persons involved (anonymous student evaluations are one example), and have proven themselves to be inept in assisting to remediate and/or remove incompetent faculty.

Chapter 3 pointed to a national study that showed the issue of determining minimum qualifications for faculty and staff still remains in the hands of the local community and junior college boards of trustees in most of the states surveyed. This type of flexibility is almost unheard of today in the common schools (secondary) where legislated standards are the norm. Chapter 3 also dealt with the tremendous problems faced by the common schools. They often have their minimum qualification levels legislated at such a *low level* that seniority status, during periods of retrenchment, far outrules the competency and qualifications of individual faculty in a subject field in deciding who is retrenched. Under such a system, many faculty are left to teach in subject areas in which they have little to no interest, very limited coursework, and often have an inadequate and outdated background to meet the needs of students. And, this all occurs in a fast-changing and recently-critized educational system.

It is ironic that the common schools in a number of states have been going through a releasing/reduction experience in terms of the number of *competent* faculty (based on seniority only) at the same time several national studies have focused on high school students' lack of preparation. The demand for students to achieve a much higher academic performance throughout the remaining 1980s and beyond is now in the process of being legislated in state after state.

Few states, on the other hand, appear ready to deal with raising the *low faculty qualification levels* that are the key to the success of these same students. This author has dealt with the development possibilities of a qualifications and competency system that demands excellence (Chapter 3). It starts with the hiring of staff and continues throughout the non-tenured period and into the tenured years for faculty and academic support personnel. The system promoted in this book grants *competency* status to faculty and others only after it is earned through satisfactory performance and an administrative evaluation system.

The minimum qualifications for any position in both the secondary school and college system need to be set high enough to insure that the *most qualified and competent* people can be maintained in their position at any time retrenchment or reduction in force (R.I.F.) becomes necessary. A strict seniority system that determines the retention of faculty in an institution strictly by length of time in the institution, without regard to the qualifications and competency issues, *must not be tolerated* by governing boards or administrators. This issue must also be addressed by faculty members who pride themselves on quality and excellence in instruction. This author believes that when properly involved and informed on these issues, most faculty members will work for the same high standards as the administration and governing boards in their institutions.

Such issues are paramount to an institution that wishes to maintain its integrity. Such issues also form the framework from which educational institutions can set up a meaningful faculty and academic support personnel evaluation system.

Evaluation begins at the time potential employees are screened and hired. Persons who may not meet the qualifications of the position initially (providing they are properly defined) may be required to do so during their period of non-tenured or probationary status. This progress can be checked and written up as part of the evaluation process which should also document all other aspects of the person's job performance.

In this book, much of the presentation has been based

on the need for educational institutions to assume an administrative evaluation system carried out by *well qualified* administrators. The author has evaluated the literature to show the gaps and self-serving roles that student-, peer-evaluation systems serve. Yet, such systems dominate the four-year college and university system as well as many community and junior colleges. While such evaluation systems may be less threatening and easier to administer for both faculty and administrators, they have not proven to provide an *guarantee* of quality in instruction.

Student evaluations are not notorious for identifying and removing incompetent faculty. Their value in identifying faculty for meritorious recognition is also doubtful when only 12 percent of the faculty in a sample of 400,000 are given rankings less than average. Peer evaluation between faculty members appears to have the same outcomes. Peers are not likely to challenge the defects and deficiencies of their colleagues or require a remediation process. Many of the peer evaluation systems documented in the literature seem to center on those aspects of the faculty member's job that can be seen or comes from heresay by students or other faculty members. Very seldom has peer evaluation involved intensive in-class evaluation procedures with some degree of objectivity.

The bottom line for both student and peer evaluation systems is that incompetence is seldom to never properly documented and removed. Using either system in a faculty dismissal would provide soft evidence for a board of trustees in a court of law. It may also lead to reinstatement of such faculty members and destroy the initiative of the board and its administrators to try such action against a faculty member again.

Several chapters of this book were developed around an administrative evaluation system that is both summarative and evaluative in nature. The "strawperson" chapter sought to identify those characteristics that quality faculty members should possess. Such qualities should be thoroughly understood by any administrator who enters into a classroom for evaluation purposes. It cannot be stressed enough that administrators who are charged with evaluation in the classroom should be (or have been) exceptional teachers themselves, and have kept themselves well grounded in effective teaching techniques and educational psychology principles for good learning environments. These qualities and credentials will greatly assist administrative evaluators in gaining the respect and credibility necessary to succeed in such a system. A well-developed and objectively-administered evaluation system should start producing the results that are expected in quality teaching and other job responsibilities.

Colleges do not have the same obligation to retain non-tenured faculty nor provide them with the same depth of evaluation in terms of reasons for dismissal as is required for tenured faculty. The "probationary" period for non-tenured faculty, if properly used to evaluate a new faculty member's work thoroughly, is the best guarantee a school administration can give itself that it will have a competent tenured faculty member for the years ahead.

Courts usually have not seen non-tenured faculty members who are dismissed as having the same *property rights* as tenured faculty members in their jobs. It makes sense, therefore, that if a non-tenured faculty member causes the administration any substantial concern about his or her teaching, or any other job responsibility, an early dismissal may be well advised. Those faculty who are recommended for tenure by the college president to the board of trustees should be the very best the college can provide. A faculty member going on tenure should provide those family's with pre-school children in a high school or community college district a *guarantee* that their children will receive quality instruction or academic support services when their children reach an age where they will attend those educational institutions.

The evaluation of tenured faculty is often overlooked and avoided by many colleges. The "protected" status that tenure provides is not well understood and gives a mystique to tenured faculty that is wrongly interpreted by many governing boards, administrators, and faculty. There are good reasons for tenure to exist. The changing of board members and administrators have caused indiscriminate firings and layoffs of faculty members in some secondary schools and colleges where tenure did not exist. It does provide a faculty member with a "property right" to a job which several years of excellent performance should provide. It does not, however, provide a sanctuary for the *incompetent or prematurely retired* faculty member. Those boards and administrators who allow such persons to continue without serious evaluation reports and/or eventual dismissal of such persons should be seen as *negligent.* In such cases, tenure *is not the problem!*

Most administrative evaluations will result in positive and supportive information for faculty and academic support personnel. Suggestions for improvements will also come out of this type of evaluation system. This author has promoted the need for merit recognition for outstanding teaching and other job performances. Such recognition will go beyond the basic needs of self-preservation, etc., that people have. The higher-level need of recognition will be met and provide the stimulus for faculty to keep producing at a high quality level. It should also provide motivation for others on the faculty to see that above-average efforts can and will be recognized.

Negative evaluations should be forthcoming for a minority of any faculty. It is not realistic to assume that because a person has the qualifications for a position that he or she will necessarily be a good teacher or will be automatically motivated to produce quality work at all times. Administrators need to identify clearly what behaviors or techniques will need to be improved for those faculty or academic support personnel who are evaluated negatively.

Governing boards and administrators need to use a due process approach in assisting tenured faculty and support personnel when they have been evaluated to have defects and deficiencies in their teaching or other job responsibilities. Such due process should include written and oral evaluation notices, suggested remediation plans, and specific required changes that are documented. This author has also suggested a formal notice to remedy in those cases where behavior and performance do not change satisfactorily over a reasonable period of time. Such a notice should come from the board of trustees and provide the instructor or academic support person with very clear statements about the defects and deficiencies which need to be corrected. There will be cases where the notice to remedy will not bring about the desired remediation of the person's defects and deficiencies. The reasons will be as personal as the individual involved. In these personnel cases, the college's administration and board will need to consult very closely with its legal counsel. Movement for dismissal is a formal process that, to properly administer, takes specific legal steps by the board of trustees. The college administration and board members will be under considerable pressure on such decisions. It should be expected that faculty unions or other faculty groups may muster support and a financial commitment on behalf of any faculty or academic support member being dismissed. Such severe action may also bring a fair degree of student protest and concerns depending on the timing of such a decision. If the action takes place in the middle of a semester or term, students may fear losing their course credit.

Arreola (1983) summarizes faculty concerns relative to an evaluation and development program as follows: "Only when faculty realize that obtaining the rewards their profession and institution has to offer is a function of their performance and thus under their control, and that the faculty evaluation and development program is a valuable tool in helping them both identify and overcome the obstacle standing between them and these rewards, will the program have a chance for success" (p. 92).

In summary, the development of high qualification and competency standards are possible for most educational institutions in the United States and Canada. The administrative evaluation system that is outlined throughout this book is a proper and responsible system for governing boards and administrators to explore, develop, and administer. An administrative evaluation system, properly carried out by competent administrators and supported by governing boards, can provide for the *excellence in instruction* that is being demanded by society in the mid-to-late 1980s. It has the potential to unleash the *recognition* necessary for the most competent of faculty members, to motivate the average to become better than average, and to provide for a *just cause* dismissal for those who remain incompetent. In all three outcomes, the students and taxpayers will receive the end result of an improved educational system. *It should be worth the effort!*

Appendix

EVALUATION FORM FOR FACULTY, ASSISTANTS TO INSTRUCTION, AND COUNSELORS

To assist evaluators who actually will be involved in the classroom observation and reports, it is important that appropriate tools be developed as guides covering the pertinent areas of classroom performance. The following evaluation form is a suggested model:

SAMPLE

EVALUATION FORM FOR FACULTY, ASSISTANTS TO INSTRUCTION, AND COUNSELORS

	☐ Tenured
	☐ Non-Tenured
Name of Person	☐ Part-Time
Evaluated: _____	

Date: _____ Bldg./Rm. Number: _____

Class, Lab, Counseling
Session Observed: _____

Name of Supervisor
Making Evaluation: _____

1. What evidence is there that the person *is* or *is not* prepared for this class, lab, or counseling activity?

COMMENTS: _____

2. Is there evidence that there is appropriate homework, class participation, and other expectations of the students?

COMMENTS: _____

_____

3. Does the person use good teaching/counseling techniques and provide a good learning environment?

COMMENTS: _____

_____

4. Does the person demonstrate an *adequate knowledge* of the subject, activity, or skill?

COMMENTS: _____

_____

5. Is the discussion or activity germane to the *course syllabus*?

COMMENTS: _____

_____

6. What evidence is there that the *course syllabus* will be *completed* as required?

COMMENTS: _____

_____

7. Does the person evaluate student progress on a regular basis?

COMMENTS: _____

_____

8. Were sound testing and review techniques used where appropriate?

COMMENTS: _____

_____

9. Are grading standards observed to be of a level expected for college?

COMMENTS: _____

_____

10. Does the person have a meaningful interaction with the students?

COMMENTS: _____

_____

11. How has the person encouraged student participation in the class?

COMMENTS: _____

_____

12. Is the person able "to get materials across" and to answer student questions clearly?

COMMENTS: _____

_____

13. Does the person use appropriate audio-visual materials in the classroom/activity?

COMMENTS: _____

_____

OTHER PROFESSIONAL RESPONSIBILITIES

1. Does the person maintain attendance records as required by the college and state?

   COMMENTS: _____

   _____

2. Does the person attend and participate in faculty meetings, division meetings, and college committees?

   COMMENTS: _____

   _____

3. Does the person maintain required office hours?

   COMMENTS: _____

   _____

4. Does the person keep current on the latest developments in his or her field of study?

   COMMENTS: _____

   _____

   _____

5. Does the person exhibit a positive working relationship with colleagues and the administration?

   COMMENTS: _____

   _____

6. Does the person keep course syllabi, college and state reports updated and completed on time?

COMMENTS: _____

_____

_____

_____

SUMMARY EVALUATION STATEMENTS AND RECOMMENDATIONS FOR IMPROVEMENTS:

_____

_____

_____

_____

_____

To be signed by appropriate administrator; also by instructor, assistant to instruction, or counselor.

| _____ | _____ |
| Dean of Instruction | Division Chairperson |

| _____ | _____ |
| Dean of Student Development | Associate Dean of Career Education |

| _____ | [box] |
| Dean of Continuing Education | Instructor, Assistant to Instruction, or Counselor |

Bibliography

Agreement Between the Kellogg Community College Board of Trustees and the Kellogg Faculty Association for the Academic Year 1982-83 & 1983-84. Battle Creek, Michigan.

Agreement Between the Los Angeles Community College District and the American Federation of Teachers College Guide, Local 1521, CFT/AFT, AFL/CIO, Los Angeles, CA, October 12, 1983, through October 12, 1986.

Agreement Between: Ontario Council of Regents for Colleges of Applied Arts and Technology and: Ontario Public Service Employees Union for Academic Employees. Toronto, Ontario. Effective from Sept. 1, 1982, to Aug. 31, 1984.

Aleamoni, M. (1981). "Student Ratings of Instruction." In J. Millman (Ed.), *Handbook of Teacher Evaluation. National Council on Measurement in Education.* (pp. 110-145). Beverly Hills: Sage Publications.

Anderson, J. S. (1984). "College Administrators: The Shoemaker's Children." *Community and Junior College Journal, 54*(6), 20-21.

Andrews, H. A. (1983). *Qualifications Handbook for Full-time Faculty and Academic Support Personnel.* Illinois Valley Community College, Oglesby, IL.

Andrews, H. A., & Mackey, B. (1983). "Reductions in Force in Higher Education." *The Journal of Staff, Program & Organization Development, 1,* 69-72.

Andrews, H. A., & Marzano, W. (1984). "Awarding Faculty Merit Based on Higher Level Needs." *The Journal of Staff, Program & Organization Development, 1,* 105-107.

Andrews, H. A., & Marzano, W. (1984). "Faculty Evaluation Stimulates Expectations of Excellence." *Community and Junior College Journal, 54*(4), 35-37.

Angell, G. W., Kelley, E. P., Jr., & Associates. (1977). *Handbook of Faculty Bargaining.* San Francisco: Jossey-Bass.

Arreola, R. A. (1983). "Establishing Successful Faculty Evaluation and Development Programs." In A. Smith (Ed.), *Evaluating*

Faculty and Staff: New Directions for Community Colleges, pp. 83-93, San Francisco: Jossey-Bass.

Baer, W. E. (1974). *Labor Arbitration Guide.* Homewood, IL: Dow Jones-Irwin, Inc.

Baker, G. A. (1983). "Seeking the Ideal: Voices of Excellence." In J. E. Roueche (Ed.), *Celebrating Teaching Excellence: National Conference on Teaching Excellence and Conference of Presidents, Proceedings.* pp. 24-28. Austin, TX: The University of Texas at Austin.

Bevan, J. M. (1980). "Faculty Evaluation and Institutional Rewards." *AAHE Bulletin. 33,* 1-8.

Blank, R. (1978). "Faculty Support for Evaluation of Teaching." *Journal of Higher Education. 49,* 163-176.

Blee, M. R. (1983). "Staff Selection and Certification Issues." In A. Smith (Ed.), *Evaluating Faculty and Staff: New Directions for Community Colleges,* (pp. 67-74). San Francisco: Jossey-Bass.

Bowers, R. G., & Brender, R. L. (1982). "A Faculty Salary System that Works." *Community and Junior College Journal, 52,* 32-35.

Bradley, P. (1980). "The Illinois Tenure Law: A Negative View," *Community College Frontiers. 8*(4), 22-27.

Brown, R. C. (1977). "Tenure Rights in Contractual and Constitutional Context." *Journal of Law and Education. 6,* 279-318.

Brown, R. S., Jr. (1976). *AAUP Bulletin. 62*(6), 5-19.

Brown, R. S., Jr. (1976). "Financial Exigency." *American Association of University Professors Bulletin. 62,* 5-16.

Caskin, W. E. (1983). "Concerns About Using Student Ratings in Community Colleges." In A. Smith (Ed.), *Evaluating Faculty and Staff: New Directions for Community Colleges,* (pp. 57-66). San Francisco: Jossey-Bass.

Centra, J. A. (1975). "Colleagues as Raters of Classroom Instruction." *Journal of Higher Education, 46,* 327-337.

Centra, J. A. (1979). *Determining Faculty Effectiveness,* San Francisco: Jossey-Bass.

Cheshire, N. & Hagenmeyer, R. H. (1982). "Evaluating Job Performance." *Community and Junior College Journal 52*(4), 34-37.

Cohen, A. M. (1974). "Evaluation of Faculty." *Community College Review 2*(4), 12-21.

Cohen, A. M., & Brawer, F. B. (1982). *The American Community College.* San Francisco: Jossey-Bass.

Cohen, A. M., & Brawer, F. B. (1977). *The Two-YearCollege Instructor Today.* New York: Praeger Special Studies.

Collective Bargaining Agreement Between the Rio Hondo College Faculty Association and Rio Hondo Community College District, Whittier, Cal., 1981-1982 (as Amended Oct. 28, 1982).

170   Evaluating for Excellence

Cooper, J. F. (1978). "The Job Satisfaction and Productivity of Junior College Teachers." *College Student Journal 12*, 382-385.

Cosand, J. P. (1979). *Perspective: Community Colleges in the 1980's.* (ERIC Document Reproduction Service No. ED 178 146).

Deci, E. L. (1976). "The Hidden Costs of Rewards." *Organizational Dynamics. 4*(3), 61-72.

Delon, F. G. (1974). *The Yearbook of School Law, 1974.* Topeka, KS: National Organization on Legal Problems of Education.

Diamon, N., Sharp, G., & Ory, J. C. (1978). "Improving Your Lecturing." Urbana: Office of Instructional Resources, University of Illinois.

Donnelly, B. (1984). "Opportunity for Recognition, Reward: Merit Pay." *Community and Junior College Journal 54*(4), 32-34.

Dubrow, H. & Wilkinson, J. (1982). "The Theory and Practice of Lectures." In M. Gullette (Ed.), *The Art and Craft of Teaching.* (pp. 25-37), Cambridge: Harvard-Danforth Center for Teaching and Learning.

Easton, J. Q., Barshis, D. & Ginsberg, R. (1984). "Chicago Colleges Identify Effective Teachers, Students." *Community and Junior College Journal, 54*(4), 27-31.

Staff. (1983, June 27). "The Merits of Merit Pay." *Newsweek*, pp. 61-62.

Educational Research Service. (1979). *Merit Pay for Teachers.* (ERS Report No. ED 166 844). Arlington, Virginia.

Evertson, C. M. & Holley, F. M. (1981). "Classroom Observation." In J. Millman (Ed.), *Handbook of Teacher Evaluation.* (pp. 90-109). National Council on Measurement in Education. Sage Publications: Beverly Hills.

Faculty Evaluation System, (1983). Polos Hills, IL: Moraine Valley Community College.

Faculty Handbook. (1983). Galesburg, IL: Carl Sandburg College.

Feistritzer, C. E. (1983). *The Condition of Teaching, A State by State Analysis.* Princeton, NJ: The Carnegie Foundation for the Advancement of Teaching.

Finn, D. E., Jr. (1983, April). "The Drive for Educational Excellence: Moving Toward a Public Consensus," *Change*, pp. 14-22.

Fleming, R. W. (Chair) (1982). *To Strengthen Quality in Higher Education. Summary Recommendations of the National Commission on Higher Education Issues.* Washington, DC: American Council on Education.

Florio, D. H. (1983). "Education and the Political Arena: Riding the Train, Shaping the Debate." *Educational Researcher, 12*(8), 15-16.

Bibliography   171

Fraher, R. (1982). "Learning a New Art: Suggestions for Beginning Teachers." In M. Gullette (Ed.), *The Art and Craft of Teaching.* (pp. 116-127), Cambridge: Harvard-Danforth Center for Teaching and Learning.

French-Lazovik, G. (1981). "Peer Review: Documentary Evidence in the Evaluation of Teaching." In J. Millman (Ed.), *Handbook of Teacher Evaluation.* (pp. 73-89). National Council on Measurement in Education. Beverly Hills: Sage Publications.

Furniss, W. T. (1974). "Retrenchment, Layoff, and Termination." *Educational Record.* 55, 159-170.

Gallagher, J. (1983, July 10). "Education at the Crossroads: Unions Urge Teachers to Take Role in Reforms." *Chicago Tribune, Sec. 1, pp. 17, 22.*

Gallagher, J. (1984, February 19). "Placing a Teacher No Longer a Science." *Chicago Tribune,* Sec. 1, p. 8.

Garber, O. (1956). "Causes and Procedures for Dismissing a Tenure Teacher." *Nation's Schools.* 58, 73-4.

Gardner, D. P. (1983). *A Nation at Risk: The Imperative for Educational Reform.* Washington, DC: The National Commission on Excellence in Education; Superintendent of Documents, U. S. Govt. Printing Office.

Gill, Donald G. (1980). *Minimum Requirements for State Certificates.* Springfield, IL: Illinois State Board of Education.

Goldberg, M. (1978). "The Faculty Member as Entrepreneur." In Myron A. Marty (Ed.), *Responding to New Missions: New Directions for Community Colleges.* (pp. 55-62). San Francisco: Jossey-Bass.

Greene, C. N. (1973). "Casual Connections Among Managers' Merit Pay, Job Satisfaction, and Performance." *Journal of Applied Psychology.* 58(1), 95-100.

Guskey, T. R., & Easton, J. Q. (1982). "The Characteristics of Very Effective Community College Teachers." *The Center for the Improvement of Teaching and Learning: City Colleges of Chicago Center Notebook.* 1(3), 36.

Hammons, J. (1983). "Faculty Development: A Necessary Corollary to Faculty Evaluation." In A. Smith (Ed.), *Evaluating Faculty and Staff: New Directions for Community Colleges.* (pp. 75-82). San Francisco: Jossey-Bass.

Hammons, J. & Wallace, H. (1977). "Staff Development Needs of Public Community College Department/Division Chairpersons." *Community Junior College Research Quarterly.* 2(1), 55-76.

Herndon, T. (1983, September 14). "Why the Schools Don't Want Merit Pay for Teachers." *The Christian Science Monitor,* p. 23.

Hersey, P. & Blanchard, K. (1972). *Management or Organizational Behavior.* Englewood Cliffs, NJ: McGraw-Hill.

Herzberg, F. (1966). *Work and the Nature of Man.* Cleveland and New York: The World Publishing Company.

Highet, G. (1976, July 21). "The Need to Make It Now." *The Chronicle of Higher Education,* p. 40.

Hildebrand, M. (1972). "How to Recommend Promotion for a Mediocre Teacher Without Actually Lying." *Journal of Higher Education. 43*(1), 44-62.

Hooker, C. P. (1978). "A Behavior Modification Model for Merit V." *Phi Delta Kappan, 59*(7), 481-482.

Hornbeck, D. W. (1977). "Statewide Bargaining." In G. Angell, E. Kelley, Jr. and Associates (Ed.), *Handbook of Faculty Bargaining.* (pp. 442-465). San Francisco: Jossey-Bass.

Illinois Public Community College Act With Additional Acts Affecting Districts. (1981). Springfield, IL: Illinois Comm. College Trustees Assoc.

Jedrey, C. M. (1982). "Grading and Evaluation." In M. Gullette (Ed.), *The Art and Craft of Teaching.* Cambridge: Harvard-Danforth Center for Teaching and Learning.

Johnson, M. (1982). *A Summary of Court Cases Involving Termination of Tenured Faculty Members.* Unpublished graduate research project, Illinois Valley Community College, Oglesby, IL.

Karns, L. T. (1979). "The Use of Faculty Rank in the Community Junior College System in Florida." *Community/Junior College Research Quarterly, 4,* 335-338.

Kasulis, T. P. (1982). "Questioning." In M. Gullette (Ed.), *The Art and Craft of Teaching.* (pp. 38-48). Cambridge: Harvard-Danforth Center for Teaching and Learning.

Knowles, L. W., & Wedlock, E. D., Jr. (1973). *The Yearbook of School Law, 1973.* Topeka, KS: National Organization on Legal Problems of Education.

Kunz, D. (1978). "Learning to Live With Evaluation." *Change 10,* 10-11.

Larson, R. L. (1970). *The Evaluation of Teaching College English.* New York: MLA/ERIC Clearinghouse on the Teaching of English in Higher Education.

Lavaroni, C. W., & Savant, J. J. (1977). "Replacing Tenure with 'Periodic Review'." *Phi Delta Kappan. 58,* 499-500.

Lewis, R. L. (1980). "Building Effective Trustee Leadership or How to Exploit Your Trustees." *Educational Record. 61,* 18-21.

Lovain, T. B. (1984). "Grounds for Dismissing Tenured Postsecondary Faculty for Cause." *The Journal of College and University Law. 10*(3), 419-433.

Lozier, G. G. (1977). "Negotiating Retrenchment Provisions." In G. Angell, E. Kelley, Jr. and Associates (Ed.), *Handbook of Faculty Bargaining.* (pp. 232-257). San Francisco: Jossey-Bass.

Mark, S. F. (1977). *Faculty Evaluation Systems: A Research Study of Selected Community Colleges in New York State.* Albany, NY: State University of New York, Faculty Council of Community Colleges. Unpublished manuscript, (ED 158 809).

Mark, S. F. (1982). "Faculty Evaluation in Community Colleges." *Community/Junior College Quarterly of Research and Practice. 6*(2), 167-178.

Maslow, A. H. (1954). *Motivation and Personality.* New York: Harper & Row.

McIntyre, C. J. (1978). *Peer Evaluation of Teaching.* Unpublished paper presented at the American Psychological Association Convention (Toronto, Canada) Report No. HE 011 959. (ERIC Document Reproduction Sevice No. ED 180.295).

McNeil, J. D. (1981). "Politics of Teacher Evaluation." In J. Millman (Ed.), *Handbook of Teacher Evaluation: National Council on Measurement in Education.* (pp. 272-291). Beverly Hills: Sage Publications.

Meeth, L. R. (1976). "The Stateless Art of Teaching Evaluation." *Change. 8*(6), 3-5.

Menard, A. P., & DiGiovanni, Jr., N. (1977). "Preparing for Unit Representative Hearings Before Labor Boards." In G. Angell, E. Kelley, Jr. and Associates (Ed.), *Handbook of Faculty Bargaining.* (pp. 58-79). San Francisco: Jossey-Bass.

Meyer, H. (1975). "The Pay-for-Performance Dilemma." *Organizational Dynamics. 3*(3), 39-50.

Miller, R. I. (1972). *Evaluating Faculty Performance.* San Francisco: Jossey-Bass.

Millman, J. (1984). "Introduction." In J. Millman (Ed.), *Handbook of Teacher Evaluation. National Council on Measurement in Education.* (pp. 12-13). Beverly Hills: Sage Publications.

N. E. A. (1973). "Draft Statement: Due Process and Tenure in Institutions of Higher Education." *Today's Education N.E.A. Journal 62,* 60-62.

Nash, L. L. (1982). "The Rhythm of the Semester." In M. Gullette (Ed.), *The Art and Craft of Teaching.* (pp. 70-87). Cambridge: Harvard-Danforth Center for Teaching and Learning.

Neilsen, R. M., & Polishook, I. H. (1983, November 16). "Academic Privileges and Academic Rights." *The Chronicle on Higher Education,* p. 6.

Nisbet, R. (1973). "The Future of Tenure." In *Change* (Ed.), *On Learning and Change.* (pp. 46-64). New Rochelle, NY: *Change Magazine.*

174   Evaluating for Excellence

O'Connell, W. P., Jr., & Smartt, S. H. (1979). *Improving Faculty Evaluation: A Trial in Strategy.* A Report of the SREB Faculty Evaluation Project, Southern Regional Education Board, Atlanta, GA. Report No. HE 012 136. (ERIC Document Reproduction Service No. ED 180 395).

Orze, J. J. (1977). "Working with the Faculty Senate in a Bargaining Context." In G. Angell, E. Kelley, Jr. and Associates (Ed.), *Handbook of Faculty Bargaining.* (pp. 504-519). San Francisco: Jossey-Bass.

Perkins, C. D. (1984). *Merit Pay Task Force Report.* Washington: U.S. Government Printing Office. Report No. 98.

Peterson, L. J., & Garber, L. O. (1972). *The Yearbook of School Law, 1972.* Topeka, KS: National Organization on Legal Problems of Education.

Piele, P. K. (1983). *The Yearbook of School Law, 1983.* Topeka, KS: National Organization on Legal Problems of Education.

Piele, P. K. (1982). *The Yearbook of School Law, 1982.* Topeka, KS: National Organization on Legal Problems of Education.

Piele, P. K. (1981). *The Yearbook of School Law, 1981.* Topeka, KS: National Organization on Legal Problems of Education.

Piele, P. K. (1980). *The Yearbook of School Law, 1980.* Topeka, KS: National Organization on Legal Problems of Education.

Piele, P. K. (1979). *The Yearbook of School Law, 1979.* Topeka, KS: National Organization on Legal Problems of Education.

Piele, P. K. (1978). *The Yearbook of School Law, 1978.* Topeka, KS: National Organization on Legal Problems of Education.

Piele, P. K. (1977). *The Yearbook of School Law, 1977.* Topeka, KS: National Organization on Legal Problems of Education.

Piele, P. K. (1976). *The Yearbook of School Law, 1976.* Topeka, KS: National Organization on Legal Problems of Education.

Piele, P. K. (9175). *The Yearbook of School Law, 1975.* Topeka, KS: National Organization on Legal Problems of Education.

Pipko, C. (1983). "STATELINE: Tennessee Governor Proposes Sweeping Statewide School Reform." *Phi Delta Kappan. 64,* 525.

Policy manual, (1978). Springfield, IL: Illinois Community College Board.

Poole, L. H., & Dellow, D. A. (1983). "Evaluation of Full-time Faculty." In A. Smith (Ed.), *Evaluating Faculty and Staff: New Directions for Community Colleges,* (pp. 19-31). San Francisco: Jossey-Bass.

Priest, B. J. (1984). "Collective Bargaining — Deterrent to Good Teaching." *Community and Junior College Journal. 54*(5), 9.

Quinn, M. R. (1978). "Designing an Effective Evaluation Program." *Journal of Business Education, 53,* 343-347.

Reich, A. H. (1983, October 19). "Why I Teach: Opinion." *The Chronicle of Higher Education,* p. 36.

Merit Pay, (1981). Research Action Brief, No. 15, Eugene, Oregon. (ERIC Clearinghouse on Educational Management, ED 199 828).

Rood, H. J. (1977). "Legal Issues in Faculty Termination: An Analysis on Recent Court Cases." *Journal of Higher Education. 48,* 123-149.

Roueche, J. E. (1983). "Excellence for Students." *Celebrating Teaching Excellence: National Conference on Teaching Excellence and Conference of Presidents, Proceedings.* (pp. 29-34). Austin, TX: The University of Texas at Austin.

Roueche, J. E., & Baker, G. A. (1983). *Beacons For Change: An Innovative Outcome Model for Community Colleges.* Austin, TX: The ACT National Center for the Advancement of Educational Practices.

Sbaratta, P. (1983). "Academic Deans: Keep the Heart Pumping." *Community and Junior College Journal 54*(3), 21-27.

Scriven, M. (1967). "The Methodology of Evaluation." In R. E. Stake (Ed.), *Perspectives in Curriculum Evaluation: AERA Monograph Series on Evaluation 1.* Chicago: Rand McNally.

Scriven, M. (1981). "Summarative Teacher Evaluation." In J. Millman (Ed.), *Handbook of Teacher Evaluation. National Council on Measurement in Education.* (pp. 244-271). Beverly Hills: Sage Publications.

Selden, D. (1978, October 30). "Faculty Bargaining and Merit Pay: Can They Co-Exist?" *Chronicle of Higher Education,* p. 32.

Seldin, P. (1980). *Successful Faculty Evaluation Programs.* New York: Coventry Press.

Shipka, T. A. (1977). "Is Peer Evaluation Viable Today?" In A. Levenstein (Ed.), *Collective Bargaining and the Future of Higher Education: Proceedings of the 5th Annual Conference.* New York: City University of New York, Baruch College, National Center for the Study of Collective Bargaining in Higher Education.

Smith, A. (Ed.) (1983). *Evaluating Faculty and Staff: New Directions for Community Colleges.* San Francisco: Jossey-Bass.

Soar, R. S., Medley, D. M., & Coker, H. (1983). "Teacher Evaluation: A Critique of Currently Used Methods." *Phi Delta Kappan. 65,* 239-246.

Steinmetz, L. L. (1979). *Human Relations: People and Work.* New York: Harper & Row.

Strike, K. & Bull, B. (1981). In J. Millman (Ed.), "Fairness and the Legal Context of Teacher Evaluation." *Handbook of Teacher Evaluation. National Council on Measurement in Education.* (pp. 303-343). Beverly Hills: Sage Publications.

Swenson, N. G. (1980). "Statutory Tenure: A Response to Erosion of the Tenure System." *Community College Frontiers, 8*(4), 28-31.

White, D. S. (1983). "Can Merit Pay Work in Education?" *American Educator, 7,* 8-42.

Wilkinson, J. (1982). "Varieties of Teaching." In M. Gullette (Ed.), *The Art and Craft of Teaching.* (pp. 1-9). Cambridge: Harvard-Danforth Center for Teaching and Learning.

Wolcowitz, J. (1982). "The First Day of Class." In M. Gullette (Ed.), *The Art and Craft of Teaching.* (pp. 10-24). Cambridge: Harvard-Danforth Center for Teaching and Learning.

Index

178   Evaluating for Excellence

E

Easton, J. A., 4
Educational Testing Service, 84
Effective characteristics of
  teaching, 4
Eroding boards' rights, 57
Evaluating:
  competent and enthusiastic
    faculty, 106
  the total person, 66
Evaluation:
  by administrators, 66
  form by administrators, 74
  form example, 163-7
  of performance, 93
  performance appraisals, 102
  questions, 107, 127-31
  systems, 51
  unannounced, 63, 87
Evertson, C. M., 4, 9, 49, 50
Exams, 12
Excellence in instruction, 58

F

Faculty:
  assessment techniques, 51
  classroom evaluation, 48
  classroom organization, 9
  colleague evaluation question-
    naire, 6
  evaluation and development
    programs, 57
  morale, 57
Fatrell, M., 2
Feedback, 52
Fifth Circuit Court of Appeals,
Firing faculty, 56
Fleming, R. W., 83, 88
Formal notice to remedy, 56
Four-year college trustees, 49
Fraher, R., 84

G

Gallagher, J., 2
Governing boards, 50, 52, 58, 143
Granting of tenure, 49, 80
Guskey, T. R., 4

H

Harvard-Danforth Center for
  Teaching and Learning, 14
Higher-level needs, 107
Highet, G., 11
Holley, C., 4, 9, 49-50
Hornbeck, D. W., 82
Hummons, J. O. and Wallace, H.
  S., 91

I

Illinois, 57
Implementation of board policy
  on evaluation, 55
Immorality, 93
In-class evaluations, 96
Incompetence, 93, 98
Insubordination, 93, 100

J

Jedrey, C. M., 12
Just cause, seven tests, 153-4

L

Law as it applies to higher education, 102
Lecture, 11
Legal:
  responsibilities of governing
    boards, 56
  status, non-tenured teachers,
    70
  support, administrative evalu-
    ation, 92
Lewis, R. L., 48, 57
Lovain, T. B., 92-4, 99-100, 102

M

Mark, S. F., 51
Marzano, W., 51
Merit:
  increases, 114
  pay, 115-6, 119, 121-2
  Pay Task Force, 114
  philosophical basis, 116